Holy Curiosity

"So sensitive, intelligent, and gutsy."

—Thomas Moore, New York Times best-selling author of
Care of the Soul

"Amy brings her uniquely lyrical style to the subject of creativity, its origins, and its purpose in our lives. This book is personal, practical, and poetic all in one, and will be a welcome addition to your shelf."

—Daniel H. Pink, New York Times best-selling author of
Drive and *A Whole New Mind*

"You know that best afternoon ever, with the rain outside, and the comfy chair inside, and the good book —a glorious, quiet revelation of a book— and the family dog sleeping at your feet? This is that book. You'll have to bring your own dog."

—Sean Herriott, host of national Catholic radio program
Morning Air™ on Relevant Radio®

"With wit and grace, Amy Hollingsworth invites her readers to listen to their lives. She is bold to embrace the possibility that the Wisdom with whom God framed Creation is the very Wisdom who yearns to create through each of us. Amy draws thread from spools ancient and modern, mythic and scientific, experiential and theoretical and weaves a seamless story that calls us all to hear and respond to the whispers of Wisdom."

—Jim Street, writer and pastor of North River Church,
Lawrenceville, Georgia

"I found Amy's book to be a fascinating mix as she examines the deeper essence of creativity. Her personal journey, insights from both the scientific and biblical realms, and the practical delineation of how to assure creativity's existence in a driven, specialized world provide a portal to understanding that everything is relevant and that creativity is our inherent nature. Amy's blueprint for how to live the creative lives we are all meant to live is clear, awakening, profound and practical."

—*Carla Hannaford*, PhD, Neurophysiologist, and author of
*Playing in the Unified Field: Raising and Becoming Conscious,
Creative Human Beings*

"Amy is one of my revered people: such a warm, good heart infused with profound spiritual insight and tremendous sensitivity to others. These qualities uniquely position her to offer a nuanced, affecting, practical, and truly exceptional work on creativity in *Holy Curiosity*. Thank you, Amy."

—Danny Fisher, writer and Professor of Religious Studies at University of the West, Coordinator of the Buddhist Chaplaincy Program

Holy Curiosity

Cultivating the Creative Spirit in Everyday Life

AMY HOLLINGSWORTH

CASCADE *Books* • Eugene, Oregon

HOLY CURIOSITY
Cultivating the Creative Spirit in Everyday Life

Unless otherwise noted, Scripture quotations are taken from the THE HOLY BIBLE, NEW INTERNATIONAL VERSION®, NIV® Copyright © 1973, 1978, 1984, 2010 by Biblica, Inc.™ Used by permission of Zondervan. All rights reserved worldwide.

Scripture quotations marked KJV are from the KING JAMES VERSION.

Scripture quotations marked NASB are from the NEW AMERICAN STANDARD BIBLE®, Copyright © 1960, 1962, 1963, 1968, 1971, 1972, 1973, 1975, 1977, 1995 by The Lockman Foundation. Used by permission.

Scripture quotations marked The Message are from The Message, Copyright © 1993, 1994, 1995, 1996, 2000, 2001, 2002. Used by permission of NavPress Publishing Group.

Cascade Books
A Division of Wipf and Stock Publishers
199 W. 8th Ave., Suite 3
Eugene, OR 97401

www.wipfandstock.com

ISBN 13: 978-1-61097-331-1

Cataloguing-in-Publication data:

Hollingsworth, Amy.

Holy curiosity : cultivating the creative spirit in everyday life / Amy Hollingsworth.

x + 146 pp. ; 23 cm. Includes bibliographical references.

ISBN 13: 978-1-61097-331-1

1. Creative thinking. 2. Creative ability. 3. Creation (Literary, artistic, etc.). 4. Imagination. 5. Imagination—Religious aspects. 6. Originality. I. Title.

BF408 H66 2011

Manufactured in the U.S.A.

This book is dedicated to my son Jonathan,
who helped me reclaim my holy curiosity,
and to my daughter Emily,
who taught me how to make it grow.

Contents

PART ONE

Unraveling the Dream

1

Introduction

It is, in fact, nothing short of a miracle that the modern methods of instruction have not yet entirely strangled the holy curiosity of inquiry; for this delicate little plant, aside from stimulation, stands mainly in need of freedom.

Albert Einstein

EVERYONE CALLED HER SMELLY Nelly, which was mean, if not apt. When she used idioms like "in two shakes of a lamb's tail" and was met with uproarious laughter, she never suspected our insincerity. Instead she would laugh too, and her head would bob up and down causing dentures to clack, and her eyes would survey the room, surprised at her wit's uniform appeal. Before the laughter could die down, someone would start a new wave (as a time waster), and Nelly, who often sat on the edge of her desk, would rear back for a more generous laugh, and her legs, already parted to accommodate a more generous midsection, would open wider so that her garters were easily visible, prompting the next wave of laughter.

Perhaps this stunt was revenge for having denied the Holy Grail to decades of high school freshmen who enrolled in her honors English classes. However Dickensian in character, Nell Davenport was a good teacher, and a tough one; in her longstanding career she had never given an A to a freshman in her honors English class. The least she could do was let her students have a little fun at her expense.

The first essay I turned in to her came back bloodied. Her red pen sliced down the right side of my loose-leaf paper to show where my margins should have been. Instead I had filled in each line to the very end with my too-big handwriting, my too-eager thoughts. My words,

3

precariously close to the edge, were in danger of falling off the page, and Mrs. Davenport was there to rescue them, in two shakes of a lamb's tail.

None of the previous teachers at my small Catholic school had cared about my margins. What they saw in me was a budding writer, a prolific poet. I was like Einstein's delicate little plant, given freedom to create. None of my poems had to rhyme. Of course, I had been well schooled in spelling and grammar; parochial schools are sticklers for those kinds of things, and one teacher, a nun, heaved chalk at us for semantical transgressions. But what was more important to my teachers than what novelist John Steinbeck called a preoccupation with "every nasty little comma in its place and preening of itself" was that my words created something substantial.[1] "There are millions of people who are good stenographers," John Steinbeck wrote in a letter to a fellow writer who had challenged his grammatical skills, "but there aren't so many thousands who can make as nice sounds as I can." Like Steinbeck, my nice sounds made up for my stray margins.

But I was in a public high school now, no longer the poet in residence at my small private school. Mrs. Davenport didn't know about my past, only that my previous teachers had recommended me for her class. And in her class, poems rhymed, commas preened, and words never overstepped their boundaries.

Words first took hold of me when I was in the second grade. My teacher then was Mrs. Biller. Young and pretty and childless, Mrs. Biller had no nickname. She did sometimes have mood swings, inexplicable to an eight-year-old, which would cause her to be very angry at me one minute and then hug me too tightly the next. But despite her idiosyncrasies I had Mrs. Biller to thank for my love of words—Mrs. Biller and a dirt-poor school. The school couldn't afford individual textbooks for our second-grade class, and so the whole of our education was dispensed by oral tradition (which meant Mrs. Biller telling us what was in the book she held in her hands). There was something soothing and womblike about those hot afternoons (the school couldn't afford air conditioning either), when Mrs. Biller would direct us to lay our heads on our desks, turn off the fluorescent lights above, and read to us. That my ears, not my eyes, were the main vehicles of learning back then was especially fitting when it came time for our first poetry lesson. "I put my words down for

1. This quote and the two that follow are from a letter to A. Grove Day. Steinbeck, *Steinbeck*, 19.

a matter of memory," John Steinbeck continued in the same letter to his colleague. "They are more made to be spoken than to be read. I have the instincts of a minstrel rather than those of a scrivener." My own instincts as a minstrel came to life that day in Mrs. Biller's darkened classroom; I don't even remember what poem she read to us, only that the words were altogether different from those that taught us about dinosaurs or subtraction or catechism. I raised my head from my desk to better catch the words as they dipped and rose, shilly-shallied for an instant, and then began to rise and fall again. I knew nothing about rhythm, meter, or flow, only that these words traveled in waves, making their way around the classroom like a troubadour whose instrument played loudest at my desk. Those who view the young mind as a blank canvas would say I received an important brushstroke that day. But it wasn't like that at all. Something inside of me said, "Yes, that's it!" and caught hold of the thing I didn't know I was looking for.[2]

I couldn't wait to get off the bus that afternoon so that I could start writing. Nothing else mattered to me but getting alone with pencil and paper. My first poems were hideous concoctions, like Frankenstein's monster with badly matched limbs. I used whatever I could dig up, insipid rhymes like math and bath, ABCs and 1, 2, 3s. They would now be long forgotten had not my father, who had the instincts of a scrivener, typed them out and framed them for our family room wall. Despite shaky first attempts, I kept writing. By fourth grade two of my poems had been published in a city magazine.

My writing continued to be nurtured by sensitive teachers through eighth grade, at which point my delicate little plant was handed over to Mrs. Davenport. Mrs. Davenport had one ironclad rule in her classroom: any assignment that contained either a misspelled word or a run-on sentence would receive an immediate F. You could dangle participles and mix metaphors till the cows came home to roost, but misspelled words and run-on sentences were beyond redemption.

Thirty years later, I still think it's arguable. My essay sentence read something like: *The subject did something or other, however, no one took notice.* The grammatical error in that sentence is the missed semicolon before however; however, Mrs. Davenport took note of something more.

---

2. I wrestled for an entire afternoon with the words to best describe the recognition I felt when I first heard poetry. Only after writing out and approving this sentence did I discover Robert Frost's observation about poetry: "[It] makes you remember what you didn't know you knew."

The missed semicolon made the sentence run on, in her estimation, and with red pen she sealed my fate with a giant F.

Math and bath, and now an F. (My father did not frame that essay.)

I had never been given an F before; I rarely even made Bs. I would have gladly accepted the missed points for bad punctuation, but I didn't deserve an F for what was in essence my failure to dot a comma. Still, the rule was ironclad, and the bestowal of a scarlet F became for me as defining a moment as when the troubadour loitered at my desk in second grade. I reacted with equal passion. From that moment on, I vowed, my writing would be less about making nice sounds and more about technical perfection; I would become one of Steinbeck's dreaded stenographers.

By the end of the semester, despite the F, I became the first student in freshman honors English to ever receive an A from Smelly Nelly. I still hold the record.

It was poetic injustice. I got my A, and Mrs. Davenport got what was left of my holy curiosity.

ROUSING FROM SLEEP

Many years later I was the one sitting on the edge of the desk (sans garters and generous midsection) before a classroom full of students. I wasn't a high school English teacher, but a college psychology professor. And I was teaching a class on creativity.

Perhaps I wasn't the best person to teach on the topic when my muse had been so easily crushed, bartered for an A and a place in Mrs. Davenport's record book. And it's true that I stayed disconnected from my own creative stirrings for a long time. The result was the same achieved by my adolescent starvation diets; after a while the hunger pangs stop bothering, dejected from their failed attempts to get my attention.

Sometimes I ask my students to guess when I reclaimed my spirit of creativity. Most think it was a twist of fate after I finished graduate school with a psychology degree. While searching for a full-time job in psychology, I took on an in-between job as a writer (since I also had a degree in English). The in-between job lasted eight years. That's when I began to love writing again, they guess.

Part of the class is discussing the different ways creativity is defined. My favorite definition is this: For creativity to happen, something within you must be brought to life in something outside of you.[3] It sounds like childbirth, and for me, that was the real trigger, not the serendipitous writing job.

Writers and painters and artists of every kind have for centuries likened the creative process to childbirth and their creations to children. The examples go back to the very beginning of life; an art historian calls the red full-flowing drapery that surrounds God as he famously animates Adam atop the Sistine Chapel a "uterine mantle."[4]

But for me it was something different; it was not the likening of the two experiences but my *response* to the birth of my first child that began to loose the stranglehold. In trying to express what I felt at my son's birth I returned for the first time since Mrs. Davenport's class to poetry, to the sounds of the minstrel. There was no other way to even attempt to convey what I was feeling. Suddenly there was something inside me that refused to be restrained by my vow to technical perfection; there was a depth of emotion so intense that to express it required taking risks and pushing boundaries, letting words topple off the page and spill onto the floor.

If a single poem had first awakened my muse, then a single poem was now rousing it from the sleep of death I had lulled it into. Seizing the opportunity, it breached Mrs. Davenport's invisible borders and took back my delicate little plant.

MY HIDDEN ROOM

I'd like to say that's all it took, one dramatic epiphany, one long overdue rescue, and my creative energy flows freely until the end of time. But there is a catch: the newborn who inspires me to be creative also requires what's left of my energy. When he is followed by a sister (whose birth also elicits poetry) two years later, there is little time to create. But eventually we settle into a routine, and I begin to write again. As the kids get older, I also begin to teach psychology as an adjunct at a local university. In my classes I am careful not to douse the holy curiosity of inquiry; I work hard to encourage the students to express themselves creatively and I try to be as innovative as possible in my approach to teaching. The department chair notices and asks me to teach a senior-level course on creativity. An

3. Goleman et al., *Creative Spirit*, 8.
4. Stokes, *Michelangelo*, 94.

entire course, just on the creative process—all because when something within me had been brought to life in something outside of me, I took the risk to capture that moment, by bringing something else to life.

The department chair also invites me to be a speaker at a leadership colloquium, my first professional seminar. I am to be their expert on creativity. But a few days before the speaking engagement, I have a dream.

In the dream I am hanging my son's artwork on the wall—just as my father hung my first poems—when I see a door in our home I've never noticed before. I open it to find a hidden room, fully furnished and completely neglected. Somehow (because this is a dream) I come to realize the room belongs to me, and I have the vague notion that it has been there all along. There is a layer of dust covering beautiful antique furniture, a stately portrait hung on the wall, and an oddly placed crystal ladle, sitting lonely on the mantle. Beautiful draperies framing the large windows are musty and worn. I don't feel bad about the dust (the rest of the house has had its moments too), but I do feel a twinge of guilt when I notice movement in the room—and discover there are animals living there. Two Persian cats, left on their own, have ripped and discolored the rug (fittingly a Persian too), centered on the hardwood floor. Then a chocolate-colored dog approaches me to tell me in a gruff voice that they—he and the cats—have not been fed while I was away. The room and its inhabitants were my responsibility, but I had been too busy getting the rest of the house in order to tend to them, to even notice them.

But now, the dog was insisting, it was time to open the room, clear the dust, feed the animals.

By the end of the dream I have recovered a bit from the reproof and have a hopeful thought, that the lonesome crystal ladle on the mantle would make a lovely home for fresh flowers or a floating plant, now that I've discovered the room. It's one of those nonsensical, dream-state thoughts, but also proof of the whimsicality of the room, where dogs can talk and ladles for scooping now serve as vases.

Wanting to add a living thing to the room may have been my first step toward contrition. It was forgivable to neglect inanimate objects like furniture, but now I knew my hidden room contained living beings that couldn't survive without my attention. Neglect had led to havoc, and worse. Living things need to be fed.

I have the image of my hidden room in mind a few days later when I walk into another room, this one filled with professionals waiting for me to dispense my knowledge. I am there because I'm supposed to know something, but the chocolate-colored dog with the gruff voice begs to differ.

I had missed something elemental. There was more to expressing myself creatively than my background of understanding—both academically as a psychology professor and experientially as a writer—had informed me. The creative spirit was not a luxury I dispatch and return to at will. I didn't have the right to barter it, vow it away, or let it sit until my schedule cleared. I didn't have the right to only scratch at its surface. It was a responsibility, a living, breathing responsibility, and a gift, as the coin in the parable—literally, a *talent*—not to be buried in the ground or stored away in a hidden room.

I had been teaching the intellectual and emotional facets of creativity, but I had missed its spiritual roots, its core. The thing that gave it life, made it move, trebled its voice. I had disconnected creativity from its source, missed the holy in holy curiosity. (Even Einstein, a man of science, had the sense to get it right.)

But now a dream was offering its help. I knew that my hidden room, like most dream imagery, was symbolic, and like most symbols it pointed back to something else. What had cast it as its shadow?

Answering that question, I soon discovered, would do more than unravel my dream; it would rescue my delicate little plant for good. Having been freed from Smelly Nelly's grasp, it was now withering from my own lack of understanding.

I knew just the place for it.

2

Lesson One: Someone There

That everyone may eat and drink, and find satisfaction
in all his toil—this is the gift of God.

Ecclesiastes 3:13

B ABETTE CAN COOK.
That's what I'm thinking as I'm mulling over the hurtful words
my sister-in-law had spoken.

Her remarks had nothing to do with cooking. The slight occurred
at a family gathering after I mentioned the book I had just completed—
suspended in literary limbo without a publisher—exacted more from
me emotionally than any other endeavor in my life. My sister-in-law responded to my soul-bearing with this thought: "Maybe your book wasn't
meant to be read by others. Maybe you were supposed to write it just
for you." It was one of those sentiments that sounded right, like a well-
intentioned Hallmark card: *Pamper yourself today. Splurge on a double
latte. Take a midday nap. Then write a book—just for you.* I didn't have a
pithy comeback at the time, but later, just after leaving (the very reason
the French call this too-late inspiration *l'esprit d'escalier,* the wit of the
staircase), I complained to my husband that writing a book for no one to
read was like preparing a feast no one was permitted to eat.

That's where Babette comes in. "Babette's Feast," first a short story
by Isak Dinesen and then an Oscar-winning film, tells the tale of mysterious stranger from Paris who seeks refuge in a small Scandinavian
fishing village. There her benefactors are two sisters, elderly and pious,
who lead a small flock of followers once tended by their late father. The
tale culminates in a magnificent feast prepared by Babette for the sisters
and their little community of believers, and while all are permitted to
eat, none is permitted to enjoy. The guests, restrained by their belief that

"luxurious fare was sinful," encourage one another to eat but not to taste, which is just a shade more generous than encouraging someone to write a book for no one to read.[1]

A friend suggested I rent the film version of "Babette's Feast" after I told her about the exchange with my sister-in-law. I didn't know much about the story at the time, except that it had become a modern-day parable and had been lauded for its wry depiction of the spiritual versus the sensual. For all its current high-mindedness (and the artistic appreciation an Academy Award brings), its inception was more down to earth. It first appeared as a short story in *Ladies' Home Journal* in 1950, likely perceived by the editors as a quaint story about food that could be sandwiched between recipes and housekeeping tips. It is a story about food, as the title suggests, but only in the way my dream was a dream about a room.

One, it turned out, would be a key to understanding the other.

When Babette first arrives at the sisters' home, she hands them a letter of introduction from an old friend: "Babette can cook," it states matter-of-factly. Less matter-of-fact is why Babette left Paris, or why she promptly faints on the sisters' doorstep. Filled with compassion for the poor French creature who has tragically lost both her husband and son, the two sisters allow Babette to work for them, as a maid-of-all-work, cooking their meager meals and ministering through food to their poor and sick. Babette's contribution lightens their load ("the dark Martha in the house of two fair Marys"), and the sisters are left to do what they do best, tending their small flock and meditating on spiritual matters.

Babette's only connection to her native France, which she fled under suspicious circumstances, is a lottery ticket, which a faithful friend has renewed for her each of the twelve years she has resided with the sisters. Perhaps, she tells her benefactors, she will one day win the grand prize, ten thousand francs.

Babette has an almost black-magic quality about her, especially when the sisters learn she may have bolstered a people's uprising in Paris by setting fires to the homes of aristocrats. Her days of setting fires, they'll soon learn, are not over.

---

1. This quote and those that follow are from Dinesen, *Babette's Feast*, 16, 28, 38–39, 44, 46, 46, 48 (adapted from the film), and 43, respectively.

THE FIRST ARTIST

Food is meant to be tasted, books are meant to be read, and if a tree falls in the forest, it makes a sound—if there is someone there to hear it. The reason my sister-in-law's comment unnerved me is that no creative endeavor is complete without someone there to appreciate it.

The needful relationship between cooker and eater, writer and reader makes me wonder when this creative symbiosis first began. Is it simply a question of ego needing the massage, or does the appreciating *complete* the creating? Perhaps to find out I needed to go back to the beginning, to uncover the first work of art, to find the first artist.

The word "artist"—like the phrase "wit of the staircase," like Babette herself—is a French import. While its modern usage draws a small circle to enring mostly painters, the word was originally used to identify practitioners of all arts inspired by the Muses: poetry, history, music, tragedy, comedy, dance, and astronomy. Later it widened its circle to include additional artisans: professors, surgeons, even cooks like Babette.

But the Muses only reach back so far, and there was creative endeavor long before classic mythology was imagined. I was looking for the *first* artist.

Some might argue, with good reason, that God was the first artist and that there is no artistry like the creation of the world itself. While the second point is indisputable, it would be an injustice to call God an artist, because an artist must create out of something and God creates out of nothing. You're more than a potter if you can speak the clay into being. God is too big, too great for the title.

But the craftsman by his side is not.

I discovered by accident that God has a craftsman by his side, as I was searching for a clue to the first artist in the biblical accounts of the world's creation. There I found my answer in a series of rhythmic couplets recorded in the Hebrew Scriptures, and it would now mark the third time poetry had come to my rescue:

> "The LORD brought me forth as the first of his works,
> before his deeds of old,"

declares the first artist, the first work.

> "I was appointed from eternity,
> from the beginning, before the world began."

Before the oceans, before the mountains, before the earth or dust, out of which man was fashioned.

> "I was there when he set the heavens in place,
> when he marked out the horizon on the face of the deep."

And when the clouds were established, the fountains of the deep fixed, the seas given boundaries, and the foundations of the earth marked out:

> "Then I was the craftsman at his side.
> I was filled with delight day after day,
> rejoicing always in his presence,
>
> rejoicing in his whole world
> and delighting in mankind."
> (Prov 8:22–31, adapted)

I had found the first artist, and her name was Wisdom.

Somehow this craftsman named Wisdom, personified here as a woman as inscrutable as Babette, is present as an artisan by God's side as he creates the whole world. She not only participates in the act of creation, she is also the someone there to appreciate it, with exuberant delight. She is the first artist—and the first patron of the arts. Creative symbiosis is born.

To mark the occasion, she composes poetry, in the form of this hymn extolling the Creator, creation, and her part in it all, and I see I am not the first to tumble words off a page in response to new life.

Sometimes called the Woman Wisdom, she is not a classical muse or even a real woman. But she is a concept so crucial to the biblical idea of creativity that she has been given a personality and a task: participating as an artist by God's side in the creation of the world and in every act of creativity that follows.

I look back to find the first time this Hebrew word for *wisdom* is used in the Scriptures, and when it surfaces, it is not personified as a woman. Instead it is translated "creative artistry."[2] The first artist, then, is also the *ability* to create art. The craftsman by God's side is inextricably linked with the craft itself. In a mysterious pattern fixed from the very beginning, Woman Wisdom is there participating each time that wisdom, or creative ability, unfolds.

2. Exod 28:3, translated by Durham, *Exodus*, 381.

It was then I realized I had met this "first artist" before. She was the troubadour who loitered at my desk in second grade; she was the gift of words left there.

GOD'S TUMBLER

Wisdom is not alone as first appreciator; God himself reveals that while Wisdom is rejoicing, morning stars are singing and angels are shouting, so evocative of praise is the creation of the world (Job 38:7). But Wisdom isn't only rejoicing. An alternate translation renders her "rejoicing always in his presence" as something more surprising: "playing before him all the time."[3]

Her rejoicing is playful and likens back to processions in ancient Egypt, where jester-like performers turned cartwheels before the gods.[4] Although St. Francis of Assisi was once famously dubbed "God's tumbler" for his own jester-like performances (his take on what it meant to be a fool for Christ), it seems he was not the first to tumble for God. At the very beginning, while morning stars and angels are rejoicing in respectable ways, Wisdom is turning cartwheels.

I follow Wisdom past her role in creation and find that when she next appears in the Scriptures, she is still creating, but this time it is the tabernacle of God. She is, rightly, the driving force behind the artistic ability to build God's dwelling place on earth, to carve out what is sometimes called his Holy Space. She lavishes her creative ability on a man named Bezalel (to whom she lends her title as craftsman), and he oversees not only the construction of the tabernacle but all the furnishings and garments within (Exod 31:1–11). Wisdom's hymn, recorded in the book of Proverbs, makes it clear that in addition to rejoicing in God's presence (feet up) she also takes pleasure in mankind, and the first record of her interplay with the mankind she "delights in" is here. The first time she works in tandem with humanity it is to create a Holy Space where God can dwell. And so another pattern is set, and the purpose made known, for Wisdom's participation in the creative acts of humans: she is there to link God with people and draw them closer together.

Through Bezalel and his helpers, Wisdom sews the garments, carves the wood, melts the gold. To shield the sacred furnishings within the

---

3. Prov 8:30, translated by Murphy, *Proverbs*, 47.
4. Ibid., 53.

Holy Space, she sets the beams of acacia wood in place, overlays them in gold, and pulls the curtains tight around them. She has built her first house; she keeps her treasures stored. Now God has a dwelling place among his people.

Wisdom continues to partnership with humanity throughout time and history, even if the result is not as grand and as honored as God's sanctuary. Still, her task is to participate in every act of creation that follows the first, with delight and rejoicing (and cartwheels). Wisdom is how God echoes.

HOLY SPACES

Wisdom is how God echoes not only the first act of creation, but also his first dwelling place on earth. The craftsman by his side continues to carve out holy spaces to store her gifts.

Babette is busy carving, too, in the kitchen that is her holy space. The once poor French creature is no longer poor. The hand of fate, which had first crushed Babette under its thumb, has turned palm side up to bear a gift. A letter arrives with the good news: Babette has won the French lottery. The ten thousand francs are hers. For the first time in twelve years, she has reason to rejoice.

The sisters are not rejoicing. They know the money will take Babette back to Paris, now that she has no need for their patronage. The poor and sick who had benefited from Babette's cooking (her black magic could enliven the sparsest ingredients) fear they will once again be subjected to the sisters' plain fare.

And it is plain fare the sisters intend to serve at a small celebration for the flock, commemorating what would have been their father's hundredth birthday. Babette beseeches the sisters to allow her to prepare a meal, a "real French dinner," and pay for it with some of her winnings. Perhaps that's how the French say goodbye: bon appétit before bon voyage.

The sisters acquiesce reluctantly. Their concerns intensify as the ingredients for Babette's feast begin to arrive from Paris, ingredients that include a giant live turtle and bottles full of the devil's drink. Babette's kitchen has become a witch's lair: "The ladies could not tell what fires had been burning or what cauldrons bubbling there from before daybreak."

The sisters have other worries, too, as old fractures among the brothers and sisters of the flock are resurfacing. Without their father's strong hand to guide them, the aging sheep begin to dredge up old hurts and old sins. The sisters fret that their father will look down on them from heaven and pronounce them failures, despite what each has sacrificed to carry on his work. The elder sister, when she was young and beautiful, had given up the love of a dashing officer who once ventured into their small town to visit his aunt, a man who could have ushered her into the velvet life of the French Court. The younger sister, just as beautiful and with the voice of an angel, had been wooed by a great opera singer vacationing in the region, who offered to make her a prima donna on the Paris stage. Love and fame had been snatched from the sisters by the hand of fate, had they believed in such a thing.

On the day of the feast, an unexpected visitor arrives, making the number of guests at Babette's last supper a reminiscent twelve. The visitor is the young officer, now a distinguished lieutenant, who had once loved the elder sister. In a fortuitous turn, he is visiting his aunt when he learns of the special dinner, and he too wants to offer his respect for the flock's late founder. But unlike the other guests, he has not made a covenant with his tongue.

The lieutenant not only tastes, he relishes. As each course is set before him, as new wine is poured into his glass, he recalls the "real French dinners" he has had at the Café Anglais in Paris, a café that boasted the greatest culinary genius of the age. The other guests, who vowed not only to dull their tongues but to silence them (refusing any discourse about the food they're not tasting), rejoin his exultations of praise with talk of the weather.

But the sights, smells, and tastes of Babette's feast begin to work their magic. The wine warms the stomachs of the small flock and loosens their tongues; the luxurious fare works like an elixir, seeping into the cracks and fusing what was once cleft. Not all of Babette's fires intend to destroy; some are meant to purify. As forgiving replaces misgiving, the guests laugh, join hands, become like little children.

The loosened tongues begin to recall their founder's great deeds and from that "the talk round the table had turned to the smaller miracles of kindliness and helpfulness daily performed by the daughters." The two sisters had not failed their watchful father after all. Someone had been there to appreciate them.

When the meal is finished, the sisters find Babette alone in the kitchen, as pale and exhausted as the day she stumbled upon their doorstep. "It was quite a nice dinner," they say, assuring Babette they will long remember the evening when she returns to Paris. Babette tells them she is not returning, for she has no money left.

But what of her lottery winnings, the ten thousand francs?

"A dinner for twelve at the Café Anglais would cost ten thousand francs," she calmly explains.

With that Babette reveals her secret: she is the famous chef of whom the lieutenant spoke. "I am a great artist," she avows, in the small kitchen that has served as her palette. It is she who was revered as the greatest culinary genius of the age, but had lost it all defending the downtrodden in Paris, fighting against those who had enjoyed her artistry most.

The sisters lament that Babette has made such a foolish decision, spending all her winnings on a single meal, but Babette is unrepentant: "Through all the world there goes one long cry from the heart of the artist: Give me the chance to do my very best."

Babette had awaited her chance for twelve years, and when resources and opportunity met, she seized it. It took all of her money, every cent she had, to fulfill the one long cry from her heart. And her sacrifice was met with this reward: There was "someone there" to appreciate it. The lieutenant, who knew the quality of the meal, was there to attest to its artistry. But he was not her only reward.

The other guests—the old brothers and sisters of the flock—depart the feast and enter the fresh snowfall outside the door, "gamboling like little lambs." The old backbiting sheep are transformed into playful little lambs, frolicking, leaping, and skipping about in the snow. They do not have the culinary know-how of the lieutenant—he knew the names of the dishes, could taste the turtle in the soup, was able to identify the wine by its bouquet—but the proof of their being the "someone there" is in their response: they tumble.

Now the intent of my dream begins to come clear. Two artists—the first artist Wisdom and her protégé Babette—have illumined an aspect of it for me, shaken some of the dust from my forgotten furniture. What was hidden in my room had been infused with a purpose from the beginning. Neglecting the room meant neglecting that purpose. The "one long cry . . . to do my very best" isn't only a desire for self-expression or even an appeal for "someone there" to appreciate it. The cry has a divine purpose.

Babette had done her very best, and it was her very best (and not black magic) that had brought God and man closer together. The intangible was made whole by the tangible. But then if God took no pleasure in the tangible, he wouldn't have bothered to create the world as his footstool or lavish wisdom on Bezalel in order to create a house for himself on earth. He wouldn't have bothered to fill my hidden room with untold treasures or to infuse Babette with the skill to create a feast that could heal fractures and carve out holy spaces where the sisters and their flock could taste and see that he is good.

That "Babette can cook" is his doing, and to prove it, Wisdom turns a cartwheel.

3

Lesson Two: Secret Rooms

The soul . . . fits
Its hollow perfectly: its room, our moment of attention.

John Ashbery

EVENTUALLY MY BOOK FOUND a home and was published (I had not written it "just for me" after all), but only after my own desires had been purified by Babette's fires. More important, it was only after Wisdom had shown me the purpose of the gift that had allowed me to write the book in the first place. With intentions set aright, I patiently awaited the chance to do my very best—and, as promised, there was someone there to appreciate it.

For some, though, the appreciation may take longer to summon, but for a very different reason: what is meant to evoke the appreciation is yet to be uncovered. It was only recently, for example, that an Italian musician discovered musical notations hidden in Leonardo Da Vinci's mural painting *The Last Supper*. Whether Da Vinci would be disappointed that it took five hundred years to unearth his veiled song is anyone's guess, and while he was not the first artist to hide art within art, he may have been the first to hide what is now colorfully referred to as an "Easter egg." Easter eggs, so termed because they are hidden treasures like those small children root out at Easter egg hunts, can be found in all forms of modern media. They can be the special signature of an artist (a wink-wink to himself or his audience, like Hitchcock's film cameos) or prizes buried in software, like bonus games or hidden song tracks (clearly Da Vinci's preference). Sometimes there are even secret rooms to reward the vigilant for their careful scavenging.

When Da Vinci's Easter egg is finally unscrambled (by converting the religious symbols in the painting into musical notes), the result is a forty-second "hymn to God" that echoes the somber tenor of the painting.[1] Giovanni Maria Pala, the Italian musician who decoded this real-life Da Vinci code, says that at first the notes made no sense, until he remembered that Leonardo practiced mirror writing. Reading the notes from right to left allowed the hymn to surface. While there is some skepticism aimed at Pala's claim, there is also some support: "There's always a risk of seeing something that is not there," says the Leonardo expert who directs the Da Vinci museum in the artist's hometown, "but it's certain that the spaces [in the painting] are divided harmonically. Where you have harmonic proportions, you can find music."

And where you have Wisdom, you can find music too. She who composed the first hymn to God in response to the original creation must feel a similar compulsion in response to subsequent acts, even if the music she inspires remains hidden in unlikely places for five centuries. The turner of cartwheels is also the hider of Easter eggs.

Copyright by Giovanni Maria Pala,
from the book *Leonardo da Vinci—il mistero di un uomo*
(reproduced here by kind permission)

It's always possible that Wisdom acted alone (she's an artist too), without Da Vinci's consent. Most likely, though, Da Vinci knew what he was doing in dividing the painting as he did, lending its features to musical interpretation. He was a musician himself (in addition to being a painter, sculptor, engineer, astronomer, philosopher, and on it goes; the term "Renaissance man" was created, in part, as a means to describe him)

1. This quote and the one that follows are from David, "Italian Genius Hid Tune?," para. 11 and 14, respectively.

and included musical riddles in some of his writings. In this case, he was Wisdom's co-conspirator.

But another architect of hidden messages may not have been in on it. Although renowned for the symbolism, some of it religious, woven into his television drama *The Sopranos*, creator David Chase scratched his head when viewers saw imagery from this very same painting—Da Vinci's *The Last Supper*—depicted in the show's infamous fade-to-black final episode. Chase responded: "The interesting thing is that, if you're creative, there may be things at work that you're not even aware of: things you learned in school, patterns you've internalized. I had no intention of using *The Last Supper*, but who knows if, subconsciously, it just came out."[2]

I'm beginning to learn, as I study her more closely, that Wisdom doesn't always ask permission; she is often one of the "things at work that you're not even aware of." Nor does she confine her veiled wares to traditional arts. She, like the Renaissance man she endows, is equally adept in both the arts and the sciences. As proof I discover that one of her scientific Easter eggs may have been buried in the work of Da Vinci's contemporary and rival, Michelangelo. His masterpiece *The Creation of Adam*, stroked into the wet plaster of Sistine Chapel ceiling, is one of the most famous images in the world, as God reaches across his newly created world to animate Adam's lifeless finger with a touch of his own.

The appreciation for this hidden gift was five centuries in the making too. It wasn't until a medical student, after laboring for hours in a neuroanatomy lab, decided to unwind by paging through a book about the great artist that the Easter egg was uncovered. It was then that Frank Meshberger, now a medical doctor, first noticed something unusual about the famous work of art. The shape of the image surrounding God and the angels—the shape once dubbed a "uterine mantle"—was another organ entirely, and it was the one that he had just been working with all day: it was the unmistakable outline of a cross-section of the human brain.

In a groundbreaking submission to *The Journal of the American Medical Association*, Dr. Meshberger carefully lays out his interpretation, showing the parts of the painting that correspond to the inner and outer surface of the brain, the brain stem, the basilar artery, the pituitary gland,

2. Martin, "'Sopranos' Creator Takes on Angry Fans," para. 5. Bob Harris is credited with first noticing and then publicizing this theory at www.bobharris.com.

and the optic chiasm.[3] He makes a case for Michelangelo's up-close knowledge of the brain by citing the artist's practice of flaying cadavers to study the human body. What is more important than determining the etymology of Michelangelo's brain, according to Dr. Meshberger, is to reveal the "special message" the artist encoded into his work: God is not bestowing the breath of life on Adam (as Gen 2:7 records) but the gift of intellect. Not breath, not soul, not spark, but *a brain*.

I would guess, though, that Wisdom, in her playful role as God's tumbler, is very much about breaths and souls and sparks. She would take issue with the good doctor and dismiss the anatomy lesson. The creative abilities she inspires are more nuanced than angel's feet as pituitary gland or thigh as optic nerve. "God is more than a flying brain," agrees one critic.[4] It's more likely that the inspiration for Michelangelo's famous work was less, well, cerebral and more spiritual. It's more likely that the focal point was not the flying brain but the not-quite-touching fingers. To support this theory art historians point to an ancient hymn—the most conspicuous trademark of Wisdom so far—as the artist's main source of inspiration.[5]

3 Meshberger, "An Interpretation," 1837.

4. Dr. Kathleen Weil-Garris Brandt, quoted in Angier, "Michelangelo," para. 9.

5. Seymour, *Michelangelo*, 93–94.

Considered the most famous of hymns and titled *Veni, Creator Spiritus* ("Come Holy Spirit, Creator Blest"),[6] the composition implores the finger of God to bestow gifts upon mankind:

> *The mystic sevenfold gifts are Thine,*
> *Finger of God's right hand divine.*

It is this finger of God's right hand that some believe gave Michelangelo the key image in his fresco. The sevenfold gifts sung about in the hymn have their origin in the writings of the prophet Isaiah (11:2–3), and when I scan the list, I see that Wisdom is at the top. Further digging reveals that of the six remaining gifts (understanding, counsel, fortitude, knowledge, piety, and fear of the Lord), there are two—understanding and knowledge—that often follow Wisdom in her exploits.

In fact, the first time I see Wisdom bundled together with understanding and knowledge is in the equipping of Bezalel to build God's sanctuary on earth, as God himself declares: "And I have filled him with the spirit of God, in *wisdom*, and in *understanding*, and in *knowledge*, and in all manner of workmanship" (Exod 31:3, KJV, emphasis added). This is the case if I follow Wisdom through the Scriptures book by book, but if I look at her presence there *chronologically*, I find that this strategic triad is paired together *before* Bezalel's endowment, in a description of the creation of the world itself:

> By *wisdom* the LORD laid the earth's foundations,
> by *understanding* he set the heavens in place;
> by his *knowledge* the deeps were divided,
> and the clouds let drop the dew.
> (Prov 3:19–20, emphasis added)

A connection is quickly made as to why Bezalel, in carving out God's Holy Space, was able to rise to such a noble task: "Bezalel could combine those letters of the alphabet with which heaven and earth were created, the implements by which God created the world," observe rabbinical scholars.[7]

So then the creative letters of God's alphabet are not one but three: wisdom, understanding, and knowledge.

From the first act of creation onward these three gifts appear to be working together, to achieve the same end. They are used in tandem in

6. Maurus, "Veni Creator Spiritus," lines 9–10.

7. Jastrow, "Bezalel," para. 3.

the creation of the world and then in the creation of God's Holy Space. Wisdom has help.

Perhaps there is something to Michelangelo's idea that the breath of life that filled Adam's lungs also infused him with the sevenfold gifts recounted in Isaiah. And perhaps three of the gifts coalesce to fulfill this one purpose, to become the implements of holy curiosity.

I continue searching and find the creative letters of God's alphabet linked together yet again, in a passage strikingly similar to the one just noted:

> By *wisdom* a house is built,
> and through *understanding* it is established;
> through *knowledge* its rooms are filled
> with rare and beautiful treasures.
> (Prov 24:3–4, emphasis added)

It is the creation of the world on a smaller scale, a mirror held up to the first act. Wisdom is using the same implements, following the same sequence, keeping time to the same rhythm. But "the earth" is now a house and "the deeps" are its rooms. As the craftsman by God's side, Wisdom knows the pattern and follows it in creating her own holy space, one that shadows the first, one that is imbued with the same purpose.

I am intrigued by this description of Wisdom's house and continue my careful scavenging by turning to another translation:

> It takes wisdom to build a house,
> and understanding to set it on a firm foundation,

begins the passage in *The Message*. No nuance of difference yet, but I keep reading:

> It takes knowledge to furnish its rooms
> with fine furniture and beautiful draperies.

I drop the book in my lap, thunderstruck by the imagery. I have seen this room in Wisdom's house before: the fine furniture, the beautiful draperies. I have seen the rare and beautiful treasures stored there, but they were covered in dust. They were hidden behind a door, in a room overrun by neglected animals.

Perhaps it is her playfulness that compels Wisdom to cloak her gifts beneath other gifts. She did draw a curtain around God's Holy Space. But now she is poised to unveil: It is this brief passage of Scripture, this description of her house, that has cast my dream as its shadow. I had been trying to understand the Easter egg hidden in Michelangelo's fresco, but now I uncover one of my own: I have found my secret room, and it belongs to Wisdom.

LESSON TWO

If my first lesson was discovering Wisdom and her purpose, my next lesson was discovering she did not work alone. It was the bread crumb trail of wisdom, knowledge, and understanding that led me to Wisdom's house, the very thing that had cast my dream as its shadow.

Still there was more to uncover. I was just beginning to put the pieces together, like my first feeble attempts to cobble words into poems after Wisdom visited my desk in second grade. What had sparked my dream imagery would also require time and effort to nurture, for it too was a delicate little plant. But in the end the reward was more than I had imagined. It was the discovery of an intricate and mysterious pattern that had been woven into the words of this brief passage, a divine plan that makes plain the way creativity is meant to unfold in each individual person and in each individual act of creativity. What I found was a blueprint for cultivating the creative spirit—in the truest sense of the word—that was as old as the foundation of the earth itself.

Something had remained hidden even longer than Da Vinci's hymn to God. In fact, it lay hidden from the time Wisdom had written hers.

4

Lesson Three: Spark of the Spirit

. . . and only the spark of the spirit will remain,
pure as when it left the Creator to inspire the creature.

Charlotte Brontë

I DIDN'T EXPECT THE Easter egg hunts of dueling Renaissance men to turn up something for me. But I had more in common with my fellow scavengers than I knew. If I had been deaf to Wisdom's hymns to God in the past, it was for the same reason the Italian musician could not initially hear Da Vinci's: I had been reading the notes backwards. If I had been unable to see Wisdom (and her cohorts) as gifts delivered by the finger of God, it was for the same reason the medical student could not: I had been focusing only on the intellect. So that I could see and hear, Wisdom had hidden the antidote in my dream.

But the fact that I was wrong didn't mean I was *irredeemably* wrong. Epiphanies can upend thoughts and beliefs, but more frequently they refine. Wisdom had pointed out the error of my ways, but she was not asking me to abandon all I had learned or all I had taught about creativity. She had plans for what I already knew. There was something to be salvaged in my bathwater besides the baby.

For the most part what Wisdom was asking of me was to shift my focus so that what was in the background could take its rightful place in the foreground. It's not unlike the concept behind Rubin's vase, a simple drawing that can be perceived as either a white vase centered upon a dark background or two dark silhouettes facing each other upon a white background. The components of the picture remain unchanged, but what you see depends on where you place your focus, on what you perceive as central or peripheral. It's called a figure-ground image and I had my focus on the wrong figure; I had been concentrating on the brain and

Wisdom wanted me to focus on the spirit. They both, however, belong in the picture.

Suddenly I find myself shifting into a new position as well. Up until now my classroom teaching of creativity had been more "flying brain" and less "uterine mantle." I had been looking at the subject matter through the eyes of a pure clinician; had I been looking with eyes of the spirit I may have been able to see God as "birthing" man (and infusing him with gifts), not just bestowing intellect. But the spirit-science divide is not a new phenomenon, and I was not the first to fall prey to it. Now that I had a clearer understanding of the spiritual underpinnings of creativity, was I in a unique position, as one reprimanded and then schooled by Wisdom, to combine both sides of the picture?

What did I have at my disposal that would allow me to reframe creativity—or more important, to rightly depict holy curiosity for the first time?

With my degrees in psychology and college teaching experience, I had knowledge of the scientific data surrounding the creative process. With my research work in television, book writing, and poetry-evoking children, I had artistic experience as a writer. And now, thanks to Wisdom's dream, I had a pattern, a place, and an alphabet of three.

It would be these last things, the images from my dream, interpreted through the filter of the first and given voice through the vehicle of the second, that would allow me to bring into focus the clearest picture of what true creativity is. This, I now knew, was Wisdom's task for me, and she was waiting in the wings, poised and hopeful that the outcome would inspire music, or at least a tumble.

THE TASK

The key to refocusing my attention had been the unraveling of my dream. But before I could unfold the pattern hidden in the dream, I had to learn one more lesson, by asking one more question. There had been something more in my hidden room besides the fine furniture and the beautiful draperies. There had been animals—living, breathing (and in one case, talking) animals. I had only understood them as highlighting the destructive nature of my neglect, but perhaps their presence was indicative of something else. Had they been there to represent what was *alive* about creativity?

I retrace my steps, turning back to the account of Wisdom's first interplay with man, an exchange that allows Bezalel to combine the letters of the divine alphabet. There may be a clue in their interchange about what it is that enlivens creativity. I read God's proclamation again: "And I have filled him with the spirit of God, in wisdom, and in understanding, and in knowledge" (Exod 31:3, KJV). For the first time, what moves to the foreground for me is this: the creative letters of God's alphabet have a *conduit*. There is a channel through which these gifts are delivered. Their carrier is the "Spirit of God."

The Spirit of God, the Holy Spirit, is closely associated with the Hebrew words for "breath" and "air in motion," recalling the same breath, the same spark that makes Adam "a living being" in Gen 2:7.[1] Before this infusion Adam is molded clay, fashioned but lifeless, just as Michelangelo portrayed him on the ceiling of the Sistine Chapel. But then the Spirit brings the dust of a man to life, as Wallace Stevens poignantly recounts: "There was a muddy centre before we breathed."[2] The Spirit clears the windpipe of mud, the air in motion forces breath into Adam's lungs. His chest rises and falls; he is alive. It is the first act of *inspiration*—literally, the drawing of air into the lungs.

The Spirit is also active in the *re-creation* of man, appearing in the story of the prophet Ezekiel, when he is transported to the Valley of Dry Bones, a battlefield turned mass grave (Ezek 37:1–14). Through a vision Ezekiel becomes a participant in the same two-step process that brought Adam to life. When God asks him to prophesy upon the dry bones, Ezekiel witnesses the knitting together of the physical bodies;

1. The words "occur in parallel suggesting a near synonymity" according to Wenham, *Genesis*, 60.

2. Stevens, "Notes," 380.

there is movement and attachment but no life. Then a second prophecy summons the breath of life from the four winds, swelling the lungs of the slain soldiers. Their chests rise and fall; they are alive again. There is always purpose in repetition, significance in echo: God is emphasizing it is his breath that enlivens man.

But this scene of Ezekiel calling upon the four winds to breathe life into the lifeless is not only reminiscent of the creation of man, but of an event directly preceding it. It recalls the Spirit of God (sometimes aptly translated the "Wind of God"), hovering over the waters when the earth was formless and empty and dark. In the beginning, the Spirit, the wind, the air in motion was waiting and brooding and ready to "transform [the raw elements of the world] into a living cosmos" (Gen 1:2).[3]

We see the Spirit moving through every act of creation, so that the formless earth becomes a living cosmos, the muddy man becomes a living being, and even slain soldiers become alive again. Once a work is fashioned (or refashioned), the Spirit breathes life into it.

It is this final lesson that allows me to see that all the elements of the creative process have been set in place from the very beginning. It is Wisdom who participates as an artist by God's side in the creation of the world and in every act of creativity that follows, and it is the Spirit, expectantly hovering, who breathes life into what is created. What is alive about creativity is the Spirit's doing.

That's why there had been animals in my dream. They were the most visible reminders of my neglect because they were the only components of my dream that were alive, that drew breath.

Their presence was there to expose something in me, to show that I had been a "mystic with nobody there."[4] It was Francis Schaeffer who noted that for many years mysticism was linked to Someone (the word *mystic* comes from "mysteries of faith"), but nowadays people want to be mystics with nobody there, detached and faith-less. Breath-less.

Or if they are attached, it is to thin air. My classroom experience had taught me that. One of the textbooks I reviewed for my class, written by a social psychologist and an expert in creativity, offered this advice for finding inner inspiration: imagine "a man with a long white beard sitting on a cloud, or a wise older woman, or a science-fiction space figure . . . And now say, inside, to this figure, 'Be my guide. Introduce me to

3. Allen, *Ezekiel*, 185.

4. Schaeffer, *Schaeffer Trilogy*, 243.

new ideas. Help me make wise decisions. Lead me to the source of my creativity."[5] It is creativity disconnected from its source. Or, worse, connected to Captain Kirk.

So when there is a spiritual component included in the creativity literature, it is the wrong spirit. The right Spirit, that which makes creativity alive, is what has been missing from my picture.

I stop and take a deep breath. I watch my chest rise and fall. I respond to this discovery, this revelation of new life, in my typical fashion, with a desire to spill words off a page. But this time I keep it brief, and fold the words into the tightest container I can find, a haiku.

> Dry bones rattle, mend
> The sinews stretch and attach
> Blow now, breath of life.

It might be better than my first attempts to link "math" and "bath" in second grade, but now I know the same Spirit quickened them both. The first poem I scribbled on paper after I arrived home from school that fateful afternoon was evidence that I was not only inspired but *had* inspired. Wisdom was not the sole visitor to my desk that day. The same Breath that had allowed me to attach math and bath had now allowed me to connect sinews to bones. And it would continue its work until I was able to piece together one thing more, the pattern Wisdom had hidden in my dream.

5. Ray and Myers, *Creativity in Business*, 37.

PART TWO

Fusing the Creative Letters of the Alphabet

5

An Alphabet of Three

"I perceive these pictures were done by one hand:
    was that hand yours?"
"Yes." . . .
"Where did you get your copies?"
"Out of my head."
"That head I see now on your shoulders?"
"Yes, sir."
"Has it other furniture of the same kind within?"
"I should think it may have: I should hope—better."

Mr. Rochester, questioning Jane in *Jane Eyre*

THERE IS SOMETHING MY mother pleads, by way of defense, when my sisters and I jokingly chide her about her mothering skills. She says: "I did what I could with the tools in my toolbox." What she means, of course, is that she did her best with what she had at her disposal, with her particular personality type and with whatever nurturing her mother may or may not have given her, divvied up among us six children. Up to this point I might have offered the same defense to my college students. But now I am fully equipped; now I really do have all the tools I need for the task at hand.

I know who the craftsman by God's side is and the true aim of creative gifts. I have uncovered the source of my dream and understand that all holy spaces are built with the creative letters of God's alphabet (and appointed with "better" furniture than I could imagine on my own). I know the Spirit that enlivens all also attaches me, making me a mystic with Somebody there. I realize, too, that despite my initial missteps, Wisdom has plans for what I already know.

But even with the right tools, I can't be a retrofitter. I can't add a new part to creativity as if it were a car or a computer that needed updating. Retrofitting is all about efficiency: when technology has advanced, the old part—the best on hand at the time of original manufacture—gets replaced by the new, improved part. My problem is the opposite; I had the new, improved parts to start with. What I was missing was the original, the prototype. And when it comes to creativity (which is rarely about efficiency), the prototype can never be replaced. It can be replicated, it can be echoed, but it can never be replaced.

Wisdom's dream had given me the originals: a pattern, a place, and an alphabet of three. But before I could decode the pattern (the mirror image held up to the first act of creation) and the place (the holy spaces she has carved out for each of her beneficiaries), I recognized there was more to learn about the alphabet of three, the creative letters of God's alphabet: wisdom, understanding, and knowledge. Once I truly understood them—as the tools by which Wisdom's house is built, as the implements by which holy curiosity is expressed—then the *process* by which they are combined would become clearer.

WISDOM

While wisdom, understanding, and knowledge are often used interchangeably in the English language, even making appearances in the dictionary definitions of one another, they have distinct roles and identities in the Hebrew language even when they work in tandem.

Wisdom distilled into its contemporary meaning has none of the liveliness or playfulness of the agile biblical Wisdom. Even when not personified, biblical wisdom has more shape than its modern counterpart, an amorphous ideal to be etched into motivational paperweights. In contrast, biblical wisdom is remarkable in its specificness. It's not expressed as a floaty virtue but as a specific artistry. Remember that Wisdom is both artist and artistry, craftsman and craft—and for me, *specifically*, both troubadour and gift of words.

If Michelangelo was right in his interpretation that the breath of life that filled Adam's lungs also infused man with the gifts recounted by the prophet Isaiah, then my specific artistry or craft was not deposited in Mrs. Biller's class. It was only stirred up then. If Wisdom had wired me for words, the spark came from the connection; until then my eight-year-old self had only, like a battery, stored the potential energy for the written word. Once connected, air in motion rushed upon me, activating Wisdom's gift within me. Perhaps that's why, despite the newness of the inspiration, there was a familiarity to the experience. "Poetry makes you remember what you didn't know you knew," Robert Frost wisely observed.[1]

But there are many other things that make us remember what we didn't know we knew; poetry is only one way. When I look closer at wisdom as the craft as opposed to the craftsman (with a little w and not a big W), I find the offerings extend even beyond the areas the classical Muses oversaw. Wisdom as artistry is broadcast throughout Scripture and expressed in diverse ways, from embroidering (Exod 28:3), to metalworking (Exod 31:6), to military strategy (Isa 10:13), to diplomacy (Deut 34:9; 2 Sam 14:20; Ezek 28:4, 5); to shrewdness (2 Sam 20:22), and even to practical spirituality (Isa 33:6).[2]

Every person has a unique avenue through which Wisdom expresses herself, and we are already familiar with her aim: to unite God and humanity. The question then becomes: What is wisdom for me, specifically?

UNDERSTANDING

If wisdom is a specific area of creativity, then the second letter in the divine alphabet is the *thinking* that undergirds that specific area, the mental processes needed to carry it out. The biblical concept of understanding is sometimes translated "discernment" and carries in its meaning the ability to solve problems. When the Spirit of God was equipping Bezalel to build God's Holy Space, wisdom was not enough. Bezalel needed a "talent for solving the inevitable problems involved in the creation of so complex a series of objects and materials," and that talent was bestowed upon him in the form of understanding.[3]

So if wisdom is the *craft*, then understanding is the *craftiness*, the mental dexterity needed to resolve difficulties and overcome obstacles. It's the answer to Wisdom's playful cartwheels in the form of mental gymnastics. This dexterity is something I'm familiar with, something embedded in the various definitions of creativity that psychology has to

1. McCrone, "Remembering Robert Frost," para. 4.
2. Zodhiates, *Hebrew-Greek*, 1591.
3. Durham, *Exodus*, 410.

offer. Some psychologists view creativity as the ability to solve problems in a distinct way, to be able to take disparate things and find common ground, to put two things together that are rarely joined in order to make something new. Alexander Graham Bell, for example, used the human ear as a model for the telephone. Bell did so by translating what he had learned from his speech and hearing studies—endeavors motivated by the deafness of both his mother and his wife—into the prototype for his "talking box" invention. This mental shift, this ability to translate one thing into another—if a thin, delicate membrane can move the bones in the ear, then why can't a larger, stouter piece of membrane move a piece of steel?—is the work of the crafty member of the divine alphabet.

Perhaps it was understanding, then, that prompted me to put a living thing in the crystal ladle resting on the mantle, in the secret room Wisdom had woven into my dream. Perhaps it was understanding that allowed me to translate a ladle for scooping into a vase for holding, carving out a space to revive my delicate little plant.

The thinking aspect of the creative process is, unfortunately, what most creativity books *start* with; they gloss over the specificness of wisdom to focus on the generalness of process. They use as their starting point a host of creative-thinking exercises as if the exercises themselves can make you paint like Picasso. It is the detached and breathless form of creativity, disconnected from its source but trying desperately to conjure up something from nothing. This is, of course, impossible, and again the Hebrew language is better at distinguishing who can "create" in the truest sense of the word. In one of its verb forms, the Hebrew word for "create" is used only with God as its subject, since he alone can speak things into being. The Hebrew synonyms for "create" that *do* allow humans as their subjects have less to do with initiating an object, bringing it into existence, and more with "manipulating it after original creation."[4] As created beings, we have to create out of something. We do that by connecting, by rearranging, by reordering what is already there. Understanding is what allows us to do that. We are not so much creators as we are fashioners and refiners. Alexander Graham Bell fashioned the telephone from the ear, but that ear was created by God and attached to Adam while he was still clay.

---

4. Zodhiates, *Hebrew-Greek*, 1583.

That leads me to perhaps the best definition of creativity I've been able to come up with so far: We express our creativity, our holy curiosity, by *rearranging the something of God.*

To rearrange God's something we uncover how Wisdom is uniquely expressed in us, mingle that expression with the mental agility of understanding, and finally, join both to the last creative letter of God's alphabet, the final member of the alphabet of three.

KNOWLEDGE

Wisdom and understanding weren't the only tools needed to build God's Holy Space, nor were they the sole implements by which Wisdom's house was constructed. There was one more tool needed: the skill to do the task at hand. That's the role of *knowledge.* The biblical idea of knowledge has little to do with bookish learning or staid erudition; instead, it is a practical skill, that which is gained through the senses, and it results in an "experienced hand needed to guide and accomplish the labor itself."[5] It is the biblical equivalent to technical know-how. If playfulness is needed to propel a cartwheel, then knowledge is the mechanics of the tumble (right hand, left hand, legs move through the air turning like a wheel, left foot, right foot). Having a talent (or even a playfulness) for a certain area of creativity is not enough; what's needed is the experience and training to develop that talent.

And so we see how fully the three letters of the divine alphabet complete each other:

- Wisdom is the *craft,*

- Understanding is the *craftiness,* and

- Knowledge is the *craftsmanship,* the skill and expertise needed to complete the task that talent and creative thinking alone cannot do.

Once equipped with all three, Bezalel becomes, as one biblical scholar concludes, "the artisan divinely endowed."[6]

But I don't believe this is a unique circumstance. The "artisan divinely endowed" is meant to be each one of us, following the pattern set

5. Durham, *Exodus*, 410.

6. This and the quotation that follows are from Durham, *Exodus*, 409, 410, respectively.

by the first artist. Included in that pattern is uncovering our area of creativity, honing the thinking skills behind it, and developing the expertise necessary to allow the Spirit to bring it to life.

"Bezalel, so gifted," the same scholar continues, "is the *ideal combination* [of qualities to] bring artistic ideals to life with his own hands." He is the ideal combination because each of the implements of holy curiosity working alone would be insufficient for the creative process. Of that I am now certain. But that doesn't mean there isn't more mental shifting to be done. Indeed, it's this mention of "ideal combination" that makes me—to rearrange Robert Frost's comment—remember what I did know I knew.

IDEAL COMBINATION

My own painful lesson in freshman honors English has made me vow as an educator never to quell the creative stirrings of my students. I have found, though, sadly and often, that students enter my classroom with their delicate little plants already squashed, and it's almost always from an experience similar to mine. Much of my calling as a teacher is to untangle and revive the delicate little plants that pass through the door of my classroom. My students freely share their own stories, and this is one I regularly pass on to them.

It's about a young girl named Teresa whose kindergarten teacher came to her home for an end-of-the-year conference with her mother. During their meeting, Teresa listened in from the next room. "I think Teresa shows a lot of potential for artistic creativity," she heard her teacher say (the same two words, reversed as in a mirror image, used to translate "wisdom" in its first biblical appearance). "I hope that's something she really develops over the years." Teresa wasn't exactly sure what artistic creativity was, but it sounded like something to hold on to.

In first grade Teresa no longer had all-day access to art materials; instead, art was considered a subject and relegated to a time slot every Friday afternoon. By second grade overambitious tasks, such as reproducing Da Vinci's masterpieces on loose-leaf paper with crayons, were assigned and graded. "I was really aware at the time that my motivation for doing artwork was being completely wiped out," she remembers.[7]

7. Goleman et al., *Creative Spirit*, 61.

Researchers have found that while most children, like Teresa, enter school with a desire to learn and explore, by the time they are in third or fourth grade, their creativity is effectively squelched. In fact Teresa grew up to *be* one of those researchers. Now Dr. Teresa Amabile, she is a Harvard University professor and a leading expert in the field of creativity. She has spent much of her career unearthing what "kills creativity" as a means to reverse the trend, this early experience impelling her to her current work as my red-pen assault by Mrs. Davenport had mine. And it is Teresa Amabile's research that was brought to mind by the mention of an "ideal combination."

Through her extensive research, Dr. Amabile found this: in order for creativity to happen, several components must be at work, simultaneously and in combination. One of these components is intrinsic motivation, which is simply the desire to do something for its own sake, like her kindergarten love of artwork before it became a graded subject. It's what you choose to do regardless of whether there is a gold star or a salary check attached. It's the bliss in "follow your bliss," and it reveals your natural bent, your potential energy. (Once I heard it put this way: What would you do if you didn't have to worry about money or status or *disappointing* anybody?)

Another thing that must be at work, according to Amabile's research, is the ability to think creatively. Along with certain character qualities (such as perseverance), this component includes the capacity to use analogies—finding a similarity of some kind between two things otherwise unlike—and the ability to see the conventional in unconventional ways.

The last element Amabile found necessary for creativity is expertise in the field of endeavor, whether that's physics or music or cooking. Expertise is the basic mastery of a field, the technical skills needed to carry out lab experiments, write music, or prepare a dinner for twelve at the Café Anglais. Together these elements in her three-component model ideally combine to generate creativity.

I had been teaching Amabile's model in my classes for years, long before my dream revealed a secret room or the trail of wisdom, understanding, and knowledge led me to the source of that dream. To dig deep into the meaning of these words for the first time only to find them paralleled in what I did know I knew surprised me. These were not merely words strung together for poetic emphasis but concepts that could be clearly defined, distinguished from one another, and even backed up by scientific data. This biblical trio was more than bread crumbs to help me find my way; they held clues to understanding the core of creativity as much as the dream itself. In the end, the creative letters in God's alphabet don't replace the tools I have in my toolbox; they don't cancel out or supersede the scientific theories I have already been teaching. Instead, they confirm them. I thought my task was to combine both sides of the picture, but I am finding they are mirror images, like the twin silhouettes in Rubin's vase. This is why there had been no need for me to retrofit: as far as creativity is concerned, nothing has been improved upon, only its roots uncovered.

RINGS A BELL

I feel a sense of justice as a sometimes-poet to discover this model of creativity embedded in the balladry of Scripture, to see poetry begetting science, to watch as metaphor cartwheels into scientific reality. The parallels are clear: How you are intrinsically motivated reveals the unique way wisdom is expressed in you; it exposes your specific area of creativity. Creative-thinking skills are descendents of understanding, the thinking-uniquely aspect of the creative process. Lastly, expertise stands as an exact reflection of biblical knowledge with its emphasis on skill and technical know-how. It more than rings a bell.

To flesh out this new discovery, I want to return to Alexander Graham Bell and his ear-as-talking-box invention. I want to look at his creative fusion through the dual lenses of spirit and science, to see how all three components—now twice established—dovetail seamlessly into holy curiosity.

As an example, when young Aleck chose to do what interested him most, to engage in an activity for its own sake, it usually involved experimenting and a little bit of troublemaking. One led to the other when Aleck and his best friend were playing one day at the flour mill run by his friend's father. The father channeled the boys' energy (and kept distractions to a minimum) by putting them to work, removing husks from wheat. This experience gave rise to Aleck's first invention at the age of twelve, a machine of paddles and brushes to do the dehusking for him. If idle hands are the devil's workshop then busying Aleck's hands led to his own workshop: the boy's father ceded a small workshop so that Aleck could continue to invent. A holy space had been carved out for him, even as a young boy.

Aleck's inventiveness and curiosity were also pulled in the direction of voice trickery; throwing his voice was a way for him to entertain family and friends without overstepping the bounds of his natural introversion. And here's where the playfulness of Wisdom puts her stamp on the more clinical-sounding "intrinsic motivation": as Aleck grew into his teen years, he transferred his voice tricks onto the family dog, teaching it to emit a steady growl and then manipulating its vocal chords so that it formed the question, "How are you, Grandma?" Neighbors came to marvel at his "talking dog"; later Aleck would manipulate another of God's creations and the whole world would come to marvel at his "talking box."

Sensitivity was also one of Aleck's natural inclinations, and it inclined especially toward his mother, who was gradually losing her hearing. Combining his affinity for sounds with his love for his mother, Aleck would keep her abreast of family conversations by sitting close to her and shaping the words being spoken into the palm of her hand, his knack for translating being used in a different way. He also created a way of speaking in clear tones directly into her forehead, allowing her to hear the words that were being spoken (not simply feel them formed in her hand). The spiritual dimension of creativity can't be missed here; the same innate bent that playfully made a dog talk also pressed lips against a mother's forehead so that she could hear. If the purpose of Wisdom is to unite God and humanity, it seems she is gracious to extend her reach to unite mother and son—and mother to the rest of the world as well.

I have already mentioned Bell's ability to translate the mechanics of the ear into the telephone as an outworking of understanding, but this translative ability was even evident from invention to invention. Before there was a talking dog and a talking box there was a talking head, a mechanical head and throat Aleck and his brother devised together. The invention used bellows to force air through a mock windpipe to say— and rightly so, given its inspiration—"Mama." Not only was Aleck transforming one invention into another, he was also unwittingly replicating the process of creative animation: mimicking the "air in motion" that first forced air into Adam's muddy lungs and continues, as the ultimate agent of the transformative, to quicken subsequent acts of creativity. Aleck used the same concept of forced air—this time across blocks of ice—

to invent the earliest prototype of indoor air conditioning. Through his creative thinking skills, he not only rearranged parts of God's creation—first the part that speaks and later the part that hears—but also echoed the process of creative animation.

Lastly, Aleck's knowledge, his skill in producing (and reproducing) sounds, was almost a birthright. His father, his uncle, and his grandfather were elocutionists who studied and taught the elements of formal speaking. His father's book on how to teach the deaf to speak, published in his native Scotland, sold a quarter million copies in the U.S. alone. Aleck was not only motivated by love of sound, the love of his mother, but he also had the experience and training—first by his father, then by his grandfather, and later at the University of Edinburgh—to bring his ideas to life. He eventually opened a school in Boston, where he privately tutored deaf students to speak according to a system his father had devised, using symbols to show the position and movement of the throat, tongue, and lips as they make sounds. One of his pupils was a young Helen Keller, who would become his lifelong friend. Aleck schooled her even in private matters, encouraging her that deafness and blindness did not rule out marriage for her. As proof, he offered his own happy union with his wife, who had been deaf from childhood (and a pupil turned lifelong friend, too). Keller never married but she considered Dr. Bell her oldest friend and would laud his unwavering commitment to transcend what she called "the inhuman silence which severs and estranges."[8] This connective tissue of creative endeavor—not severing but joining, not estranging but uniting—continued to hallmark Aleck's life and work.

Aleck persisted in his attempts to find new ways to help the deaf hear through electronic devices, and all the while the telephone was being conceived—as a byproduct of a system that helped his students "see" sounds they could not hear.[9] At one point he became stuck in the creative process, as he tried to transmit the human voice by telegraph, and while visiting the director of Smithsonian Institution, Aleck told him he didn't have the knowledge of electricity needed to complete his task. "Get it!" the director shouted.[10] Blustered into persevering and with funding from his father-in-law, Aleck hired an electrical designer and mechanic, a young man named Watson (as in the now famous "Mr.

8. Harrity and Martin, *Three Lives of Helen Keller*, 103.

9. Ibid., 28.

10. Harlow, *Old Wires and New Waves*, 355.

Watson, come here. I want to see you."). With Aleck's wisdom and motivation, his thinking skills, and the collaborative knowledge of Bell and Watson, the telephone came to life.

When Aleck died at age seventy-five, having also invented such varied things as the metal detector and an iceberg locator, it was the telephone that brought him the most acclaim. On the day of his burial, all telephones in his adopted homeland of America ceased their ringing for one minute in homage to his life's work, and the man who made sound possible for the deaf received his thanks in silence.

It seems he left this world without a sound as well. When on his deathbed his wife had whispered in his ear, "Do not leave me," words he had taught her to speak, his final word to her—"no"—was not spoken but signed. One last translation of words through his fingers and he was gone. The lips that pressed against his mother's forehead silenced, the hand that signed his final word to his wife stilled, Alexander Graham Bell left the earth having completed his task, ideally.

6

Letter One: Many Reflections

Raphael paints wisdom; Handel sings it, Phidias carves it,
Shakespeare writes it, Wren builds it, Columbus sails it,
Luther preaches it, Washington arms it, Watt mechanizes it.

Ralph Waldo Emerson

LIKE EINSTEIN, I WEAR the same clothes everyday when I work. For him, wearing the same threadbare sweater and old-man pants day after day was a way to conserve his mental energy and free his mind to solve the world's mysteries. Why waste brain power deciding what to wear? For me, the blue nylon jogging pants (singed by a coffee mug on one knee) and the faded Mary Washington College t-shirt (it became a university years ago) just mean comfort during the long hours writing at the computer. My motivation is more leisure than lofty. But loftiness must have worked for Einstein; he at least understood that creative gifts were not bestowed by a flying brain. He had the sense and reverence to call them holy.

But what is holy needs a practical outlet as much as what is scientific. It's not enough to know that every person is endowed with wisdom, a specific area of creativity, and that wisdom is manifested through an internal—and scientifically verifiable—bending toward one area and not another. To know that biblical wisdom is remarkable in its specificness means nothing unless this question is answered: What is wisdom for me, specifically? And if wisdom is splayed in many different directions, both metaphorically and scientifically, how do I know which reflection is mine?

A practical way to identify wisdom's many reflections might be to study the habits and behaviors of very creative children, those too young to have encountered a Smelly Nelly, those yet to be handed Da Vinci and crayons. If the spark comes from the connection and most of these connections are made in childhood, perhaps it's best to look at those with their delicate little plants still intact. And yet the scientist who attempted to do so found the real breakthrough came from an unexpected source: it was not from a lab filled with curious young minds, but from a medical center filled with brain-damaged adults. It was, in fact, the juxtaposition of working with two such dissimilar groups that led to one of the greatest contributions to the understanding of creativity in the twentieth century. While researching stroke victims in the morning and artistic children in the afternoon, Howard Gardner, a Harvard psychologist who also taught neurology at Boston University, found that both groups "were clueing me into the same message: that the human mind is better thought of as a series of relatively separate faculties, with only loose and nonpredictable relations with one another, than as a single, all-purpose machine."[1]

One of Gardner's "clues" was the fact that while some of the stroke victims suffered from aphasia (the inability to speak or understand words after brain injury), they were not necessarily impacted in other areas. Yet those stroke victims who did retain the ability to speak and understand language were unable to do other things, like sing a song or relate to others socially. From the gifted children Gardner learned that while some were exceptionally creative in certain areas, they were quite ordinary in others; there was no such thing as across-the-board creativity. Their strengths were uneven, skewed. How were these scenarios possible if intelligence is uniform, if the brain operates as a "single, all-purpose machine"?

Lopsided strengths are hard to explain, and in any case, *either/or* thinking had sufficed for a long time: a person is *either* smart *or* stupid; a person is *either* creative *or* hopelessly unimaginative. An IQ secured one's place in the universe, making it impossible to cross the genetic divide. Should one try, like the fictional Charlie Gordon, the once mentally retarded janitor turned super genius in *Flowers for Algernon,* fate will see to it you are returned to where you belong. Intelligence has its own caste system. Gardner challenged this thinking, instead proposing that the brain consisted of "separate faculties," which showed themselves in a variety of ways, like wisdom's many reflections. He called these faculties "intelligences" to dispel the long-held belief that intelligence was a one-dimensional phenomenon. (His theory is commonly synthesized

1. Gardner, *Intelligence Reframed*, 32.

into, "It's not how smart you are, but how you are smart."[2]) Based on his continued research with both adult stroke victims and gifted children, Gardner uncovered seven intelligences, seven "hows" or kinds of smart:

> **Musical**: This intelligence involves skill in the performance, composition, and appreciation of musical patterns and can be seen in musicians and composers.
>
> **Bodily-kinesthetic**: Involves using one's whole body or part of the body (e.g., hand or mouth) to solve problems or fashion products. Obvious examples include dancers, actors, and athletes; less obvious, craftsmen, surgeons, and mechanics.

One of my college students who scored high in this intelligence described its expression as the source of much chagrin in kindergarten, where he was forced to give up recess (the very thing he needed) because of his inability to sit "still" and learn.

> **Spatial**: Involves the ability to recognize and manipulate the patterns of wide spaces as well as the patterns of more confined areas. Those who operate wide spaces include navigators and pilots; those who manipulate more confined spaces include sculptors, chess players, and architects.

Gardner called these next two intelligences the personal intelligences. Although each of the intelligences has an emotional component, these two are the most firmly rooted in emotional perception.

> **Interpersonal**: Involves the capacity to understand the intentions, motivations, and desires of other people, resulting in the ability to work effectively with others, as do salespeople, teachers, religious leaders, and politicians.
>
> **Intrapersonal**: Involves the ability to understand oneself, one's own desires, fears, and capacities and using that understanding to effectively regulate one's life. This intelligence is evident in philosophers, psychologists and theologians.

And, of course, Gardner includes these two, the only two *traditionally* linked to intelligence:

> **Linguistic**: Involves sensitivity to spoken and written language, the ability to learn languages, the capacity to use language to ac-

---

2. The descriptions of the intelligences that follow are adapted from Gardner, *Intelligence Reframed*, 41–43.

complish certain goals. This intelligence can be seen in lawyers, speakers, and writers.

Logical-mathematical: Involves the capacity to analyze problems logically, carry out mathematical operations, and investigate issues scientifically. It also includes the ability to detect patterns, using logic and numbers to make connections and understand information. This intelligence can be seen in mathematicians, scientists, and economists, and also in researchers and detectives.

My Uncle Milton, whose mental capacity because of brain damage at birth resembles Charlie Gordon's, nevertheless has astonishing mathematical skills. He was never officially diagnosed a savant, but he could add up the grocery items in his head and tell you the total before the cashier could mechanically do so. As kids, we would quiz him with mercilessly long equations, and he was still quicker than our nimble fingers on the calculator.

Gardner's theory of multiple intelligences, introduced to the academic world in 1983, naturally transformed how educators viewed learning and instantly liberated students who did not excel in the two areas school settings value most, language and math. (Gardner deftly points out that most intelligence tests are devised by scientists who excel in these two intelligences, which accounts for their being used as the exclusive barometers of smartness.) For this reason, I make a point to ask my students—in every college class I teach regardless of subject matter—to take a multiple-intelligences assessment that gives them a clearer picture of their "skewed strengths." While everyone has the potential for all seven intelligences and each intelligence can be strengthened, most people have two or three that clearly stand out, with varying degrees of remarkability in the remaining intelligences.

Given the newness of Gardner's findings and the time required to overturn hundreds of years of standardized thinking, I suspected that most of my students would rate highest in the traditional intelligences, since these intelligences form the core of most college entrance exams. Instead the majority of my students rated highest in intrapersonal intelligence, a hallmark of self-learners. They must have succeeded in the world of traditional intelligence by teaching themselves through the avenues of their other intelligences. One student who had struggled in math in grade school was only able to learn her multiplication tables once she set them to the rhythm of "Swing Low, Sweet Chariot." All kinds of secrets pour out about their creative adaptive skills, not only with music, but with movement and drawing as well. There is also some remorse, when they discover that at times their natural inclinations have been bent to conform, forcing their square peg to fit into a round hole when a square peg was what they were intended to be. They remember times when they have shown promise in an area but that promise has been crushed or never given the proper nurturing to thrive. Others have a vague notion something has been left untapped, that their memory hasn't yet been jogged to remember what they didn't know they knew.

Of course, tools designed to identify a person's strengths—in intelligence or creativity or any area—are ubiquitous and oftentimes ridiculous. Gardner's theory is not a gimmick; even though it is a reaction to the scientists who first narrowly defined intelligence, it is a product of science itself. His way of determining strengths is not based on silly quizzes that reveal what kind of animal you are or even (as one creativity textbook suggested) how well you can conjure up cloud-sitting sages. It's not detached.

And because his theory was born of his research in creativity, it makes a seamless transition to that field as well. "Creativity isn't some kind of fluid that can ooze in any direction," clarifies Gardner. "The life of the mind is divided into different regions . . . like math, language, or music." Because of this, "a person isn't creative in general. You can't just say a person is 'creative.' You have to say he or she is creative in X, whether it's writing, being a teacher, or running an organization. People are creative in something."[3]

CREATIVE IN X

What X is for each person corresponds to his or her most dominant intelligence: it's not how creative are you, but how are you creative. That means X can be musical, like George Handel's singing; it can be bodily, like Christopher Wren's skill in building; or it can be spatial, like Christopher Columbus's sailing, Raphael's painting, and Phidias's carving. X can be interpersonal, like George Washington's skill as a military leader, or intrapersonal, like Martin Luther's introspection that led to reform. X can be put in writing, like William Shakespeare's timeless son-

3. Goleman et al., *Creative Spirit*, 26–27.

nets, or factored out mathematically, like the tinkering that led to James Watt's steam engine.

In a poetic twist, all of Gardner's original intelligences are account-ed for in Emerson's artistic roll call that opens this chapter and predates Gardner's theory by 110 years. What Emerson knew intuitively Gardner deduced scientifically. The intelligences also bear a strong resemblance to the muses of classical mythology, each of whom inspired a different area of art or science, from dance (bodily-kinesthetic) to astronomy (logical-mathematical). The Muses served as patrons of their particular domains, and perhaps they are the guardians of Gardner's "separate fac-ulties" as well.

But, of course, the Muses are shadows cast by another source of inspiration, one that precedes them in time and history. Who is the true guardian of these domains of creativity, these divisions of labor in the mind? It is Emerson, the philosopher and poet, who gets it right this time. The source of all creative expression, he writes, is *wisdom*. He knew that creative artistry was linked to wisdom, with different artists express-ing it through different avenues. Wisdom is what Raphael paints and Luther preaches. Wisdom is what Columbus sails and Wren builds.

Of course, this doesn't negate Gardner's findings. It bolsters them. Wisdom is expressed in as many ways as Gardner has uncovered in his neurological research. Gardner is *rearranging* what is already there, re-fining and undergirding what the mythologists also tried to order. But before them all, at the very beginning, was the craftsman by God's side. She, as the first patron, endues both the arts and the sciences, so that mathematical equations reflect the heavens as clearly as a Renaissance painting. Those who come after her are only reworking the ideas and images already encapsulated in the single (but many reflected) Hebrew word for wisdom. It is the word used to describe Bezalel's skill in design, metalwork, and stone cutting and also to highlight Joshua's aptitude in diplomacy. It is the word used of Daniel's ability to understand the sci-ences of the Babylonians and also to disclose how he interpreted their dreams. Gardner may have intended to replace the old with the new and improved, but he was only echoing. Echoing brilliantly, but echoing nonetheless.

Even so, his work is a unique and appreciated display of his own "creative artistry," his own distinct blend of intelligences, at once *reflect-ing* and *exposing* the many facets of wisdom.

Wisdom takes delight in this display, as she does every act of creation since the first, and in Gardner's immense contribution to helping others discover their own unique channels of creativity. She just prefers that he, like Emerson, had given her the proper footnote.

NO ONE SINGS DA VINCI'S SONGS

"People are creative in something," Gardner had said, and that something is Wisdom's doing. That's why I wasn't surprised when I took my first multiple-intelligences assessment, along with my first class of students, and Wisdom's gift to me rose to the top. There it was in black and white, with a percentage attached: I was skewed linguistically. But Gardner believes that most people have two or more intelligences that work together to give them their creative pulse (e.g., an actor might rate high in the bodily-kinesthetic and interpersonal intelligences), with one of those intelligences often appearing slightly mismatched with the others. Freud, for example, displayed the logical-mathematical intelligence typical of scientists, but also the linguistic and personal intelligences that made him popular with the public and resented by his less gregarious scientific peers. My results were slightly mismatched too. Since I had been a lifelong sufferer of math anxiety (a diagnosis routinely meted out to girls at my elementary school along with our seat assignments), I was shocked to find my second highest score was in logical-mathematical. But I also knew that from an early age my understanding of the universe came through finding connections between and patterns among its many constituent parts. I was a puzzle solver, a pattern maker, a would-be detective. My third highest score was in the intrapersonal intelligence, which explains my draw to psychology in college, a move that brought chagrin to my English professors, who wanted me to focus on literature only, and excitement to my psychology professors, who hoped I would bring good writing to a field that often lacked it.

One of my lowest scores was in the musical intelligence, which comes as no surprise to my husband, who jokingly calls any version of a song I sing a "remix." He marvels at my inability to differentiate notes, which may also shed light on why I struggle to pronounce some words, either because I don't hear the differences in vowels sounds or because I put the accent on the wrong syllable. One of my best resources is Merriam-Webster's online dictionary, which mercifully gives an audio version of each word in its repository. I might have to listen to the word a half a dozen times before I can assimilate it. Gardner's assessment, then, clarified two things for me: I love words, and I have trouble pronouncing them.

But musical intelligence was not at the very bottom of my list. That honor went to bodily-kinesthetic, a revelation that absolved me of many miserable afternoons in the outfield, praying that no softballs would come my way for fear of breaking my glasses yet another time. I hated sports as a kid (except for swimming) and always felt it was some defect in my character that made me not like to move around a lot or at least with more grace. It was a trick of the universe that I could feel so competent in the classroom and so clunky at recess. I had a longtime friend with the opposite problem, excelling in every sport she tried but feeling out of sorts in the classroom. She thought she wasn't very smart, but she was remarkably so, in a way that I was not.

It was as liberating to have my weaknesses laid bare as it was to have my strengths affirmed. It relieved me of the burden of thinking I had to be good at everything in order to be considered good at something. Suddenly I was transported back to that spring afternoon in seventh grade when I tried out for cheerleading but failed to make the squad. I slunk back to an empty classroom in tears to gather my books to go home only to find a note on my desk: I had won first place in a school-wide slogan contest. What I once deemed a consolation prize I now see as a clarification: So you couldn't do a Herkie, Amy, but you can string words together pretty well. There's more than one way to elicit a cartwheel.

No one is an across-the-board anything—not even Da Vinci, the mold from which the Renaissance man was cast. He may have written music (even embedding a hymn in his painting), but nobody, Gardner reminds us, sings his songs. Thomas Edison was a bad speller. Do we lament this shortcoming each time we flip on the light switch? Because the intelligences are separate entities, no one excels in them evenly.

Of course, each intelligence can be strengthened, and I have the *potential* to be a better athlete (I did make the cheerleading squad the following year), just as Edison had the potential to be a better speller. But I also know where my strengths lie, and where Wisdom has left her deepest imprint.

That's why when I review my list, I begin to understand more clearly the reasoning behind Wisdom's task for me. She knew that as an intrapersonal, I would ponder the significance of a dream. She knew that as a logical-mathematical, I would begin to see the dream as part of a larger pattern. And most important, she knew that as a linguistic, I would feel compelled to express what I found in words.

THE NATURAL

Since Gardner's theory was originally published, he has considered adding two new intelligences to his list; one made the cut, the other didn't. Each prospective intelligence is judged by eight criteria, yardsticks drawn from the biological sciences, logical analysis, developmental psychology, and traditional psychological research. The eighth intelligence to meet these standards is called the *naturalist intelligence.* As the name suggests, the naturalist intelligence involves an understanding of the living world and the ability to recognize and classify the components of the environment. It also includes the skill to care for or interact with living creatures. While most apparent in biologists and environmentalists, the naturalist intelligence can also be seen in farmers, gardeners, and cooks. Gardner was persuaded to consider the naturalist intelligence when he discovered it could be isolated by brain damage, finding that some individuals retained the ability to identify inanimate objects but lost the ability to recognize living things (or the reverse problem) after brain damage.

Gardner believes the pattern-recognizing skills found in other intelligences—those displayed by artists, poets, and mathematicians—may be built on the perceptual skills of this intelligence. So from Emerson's hall of fame of wisdom-keepers, Raphael, Shakespeare, and Watt may be among those who depend on this intelligence in their own fields of artistry. But if I were to add another member to Emerson's esteemed list to represent this intelligence, I know just who it would be: the African-American agriculturalist considered one of the greatest scientific minds of the twentieth century, who among other things discovered three hundred uses for the peanut. Giving the Peanut Man his due, I would write: George Washington Carver shells wisdom.

THE ONE THAT GOT AWAY

There is one last intelligence that Gardner has considered and dismissed: the spiritual intelligence. The first problem Gardner encountered with this intelligence was trying to define "spiritual," which he found to be a conceptual hodgepodge that included the mind, the self, the supernatural, or nothing at all. Should "spiritual" be defined as a concern for life-and-death issues, held up as a transcendent state of being, or measured by a person's impact on others? Gardner expressed his frustration that things of the spirit were not as straightforward as the domains of math and science, which are "delimited" and "uncontroversial."[4]

Given that spiritual things *are* unlimited and controversial and admitting his own lack of involvement in the spiritual realm, Gardner opted for the word "existential," which had a stronger cognitive backbone. Thus the existential intelligence would encircle only one element of the spiritual, the capacity to reflect on life-and-death issues. This concern for cosmic issues, for humanity's place in "the big picture," isn't limited to religious leaders or philosophers, although it is certainly apparent in these fields. It can also be seen in a physicist like Einstein, pondering the world's mysteries in his threadbare sweater and old-man pants.

Still, Gardner shies away from adding this intelligence to his list, quipping that he may give it status as a half-intelligence. I think in the end he was much like the medical student—and myself initially—only able to see a flying brain rushing to bestow intellect on an insensate Adam.

But I don't disagree with Gardner's decision to exclude this intelligence, not since I've come to understand Wisdom's dream. It would be an injustice (or worse) to define the spiritual as a "separate faculty" in the brain, to tack it on to a list as an additional member instead of honoring it as the breath that enlivens all.

As a neuropsychologist, Gardner viewed the intelligences as neural potentials that had to be activated by culture, like my fated exposure to poetry in second grade. I had also viewed this activation as a natural process, but now see that creative gifts are blown upon by the Spirit of God.

The Spirit then, pervading and seeping as it does, refuses to be categorized as an intelligence or even one of Wisdom's many reflections. Instead it is the Spirit—and not culture—that activates these very gifts, and stirs them to life.

---

4. Gardner, *Intelligence Reframed*, 55.

PRACTICAL WISDOM

Gardner understands it would be hypocrisy to devise a standardized test to determine multiple intelligences when his theory exposed the constraints imposed by these tests. Instead, he suggests the key to uncovering an intelligence (or a mix of intelligences) is observation by a trained eye or even the testimony of family and friends. Set a child loose in a museum, and you will easily find where his capacities lie. But it's not as easy to set an adult loose in a museum, and Gardner understands that assessments can be helpful. For that reason I am including one that he obliges, with the disclaimer that it serve as a guide only.

- To find out what amalgam of intelligences is yours, take the Rogers Indicator in the Resource Section. While observation is the best way to determine "how you are creative," this assessment will give you a snapshot of your unique combination of gifts.

- Look at the corresponding careers—or using my terminology, the corresponding "crafts"—that match up with your highest scores to find out what creative outlets match your intelligences.

This is the most practical way I've found to determine how you are internally motivated toward one area of creativity or another. But more important, it reveals the unique avenue through which Wisdom expresses herself in you, with the ultimate purpose of uniting God and man. It's your wisdom, specifically.

7

Letter Two: Merging the Creative Personality

The test of a first-rate intelligence is the ability to hold two opposed ideas in the mind at the same time, and still retain the ability to function.

F. Scott Fitzgerald

MIKE SLIPPED INTO MY classroom late on the worse day possible. The other students were all standing, which made the classroom feel much smaller (an unwelcome feeling when you're late), and not just standing but lifting their right knees up to meet their left hands, then their left knees up to meet their right hands. The braver ones tried it backwards, heel to hand. Again and again their arms and legs moved in this crisscross motion, as if they were taking a sophisticated sobriety test. And I was up front, orchestrating the drunks.

Mike, ever the obedient student, hurried to his desk and joined in.

"Activity is the only road to knowledge," George Bernard Shaw wrote.[1] He most likely meant that you learn more by doing than by being schooled (he also famously said, "He who can, does; he who cannot, teaches"), but he would be just as right in saying that you learn by *moving*, by the simple physical activity of being in motion. That's why in all my classes I devote at least one lecture to the necessity of activity, to the importance of movement in learning. It's not a new idea; the ancient Greeks schooled in motion, waxing philosophic as they strolled along the colonnades of Lyceum. They didn't sit and absorb; they walked and ruminated.

Shaw would be happy to know that my understanding of the activity-knowledge (or movement-learning) connection, a concept doubly important when creating, wasn't something I was taught in a classroom. My students would not be willing to look stupid crisscrossing in unison,

1. This and the following quote are by Shaw, *Man and Superman*, 230.

55

and the other things I ask them to do, just because I give them a com-
pelling scientific argument for it (although I do). What moves them is
what moved me; the fact that this simple series of exercises unlocked the
world of a little girl I knew and loved.

A little girl whose birth inspired a poem.

SPLIT IN TWO

If wisdom, the first letter of the creative alphabet, is best identified
by the eight regions of the brain, then understanding, the second letter, is best illustrated by a brain split in two. Not psychologically, but
hemispherically.

The dual hemispheres of the brain don't have the descriptive distinction of Gardner's multiple intelligences (it's easy to figure out where
musical intelligence shines) but are differentiated only by location: left
or right. The left brain is neat and tidy and alliterative: it deals with
logic, language, and linear patterns. The right brain is messier with its
free-flowing emotions and keen intuition and big-picture thinking. For
that reason, the right brain is heralded, loudly and often, as the seat of
creative ability.

Perhaps even more misleading than the notion that only one side
of the brain stirs up creativity is the myth of the creative personality.
When abstract expressionism prevailed in the 1960s, for example, the
art students deemed most creative by their teachers were those who
were moody and antisocial.[2] These dark artists, donning the aspect of
the brooding melancholy made famous by Lord Byron a century before,
were encouraged, rewarded, and sent out to a world that required more
than a sullen disposition to succeed. They failed because they and their
mentors believed that exhibiting (or worse, mimicking) a certain personality type is what makes an artist creative.

But the creative personality isn't shrouded in black and combing
the moors any more than it is housed in the right side of the brain only.
Wisdom is playful, not burdensome; she does not drive to madness those
she endows, as if that were the exchange rate for genius, like some soul-
pact with the devil. Poet Mark Strand likewise rejects the image of the
fragile, despondent artist living close to the edge: "[The myth is that the
artist is] so responsive to the world around him, so sensitive, so driven to

2. Csikszentmihalyi, *Creativity*, 56.

respond to it, it's almost unbearable. That he must escape through drugs or alcohol, finally suicide [because] the burden of consciousness is so great. But the burden of consciousness is great for people who don't— you know—want to kill themselves."[3]

Byronic sulkers and divine madness are more mythology than psychology; the creative personality is rarely so one-dimensional. Psychology professor and author Mihaly Csikszentmihalyi, whose study of creativity has spanned forty years, found that trying to compile a list of traits to define the creative personality (as in, all creative people are introverts) rings false. His extensive research, with creative people from every field, shows that *either/or* distinctions reveal only half the picture. The full picture is that the creative personality is remarkable in its complexity, in its ability to embrace the full repertoire of human emotions and traits, to put some of its eggs in every basket. Instead of displaying one trait over another on a continuum (e.g., imaginative at one end vs. realistic at the other), the creative personality can fully embrace either extreme depending on the circumstance. This doesn't mean that creative people shift wildly from one end of the continuum to the other; instead, they have equal access to both sets of traits and can evince them free of internal struggle.

But that's not the case for most of us. We do struggle with displaying opposing traits because we want a consistent picture of who we are and prefer to think, "I am this and not that." We choose sides not due to innate personality—these are traits present in all of us—but because we are taught to view some traits as "good" and some as "bad." In our culture, for example, independence is extolled, dependence viewed as a sign of weakness. But the creative personality understands that while independent thinking is crucial to the creative process, so is a dependence on others, especially those who have blazed the trail to make significant contributions to a particular area of artistry. Sometimes the dependence is concurrent: Alexander Graham Bell's dependence on Watson's knowledge of electricity made him more creative, not less so; had he insisted on independence only we might still be talking through tin cans attached to string. Culturally, we also tend to value discipline over playfulness, so much so that children, whose work should be play, are as overscheduled as their parents. And yet the creative personality embodies both: the playfulness that doesn't take itself too seriously and

3. Ibid., 74.

is willing to kick around novel ideas and the discipline to test those ideas and to bring them to life.

Even a set of traits that *are* attributed to innate personality—introversion and extroversion—appear to be comfortably twined in the creative personality. That's why the dark artists of the sixties failed; their introversion wasn't enough. They needed to sell themselves, get out there to be seen and heard. Romanticizing a malcontent may quicken the pace of a Gothic novel (or a Batman film), but is less successful at moving things along in the real world.

For the creative personality, then, it is not the distinction of *either/or*, but the inclusion of *both/and*. Csikszentmihalyi found that highly creative people, at the same time or at different times depending on the situation, are both imaginative *and* realistic; both able to suffer pain (truly, not as payment or for show) *and* able to experience great joy (in the creative process as well as in other areas of life); both given to high energy *and* able to draw back and rest; both passionate *and* objective; both cautious *and* risk-taking; both humble *and* able to take pride in their accomplishments; both smart *and* naïve. Gardner calls this last set of conflicting traits wisdom and childishness, but we know that biblical Wisdom admits no such conflict.

What's important about Csikszentmihalyi's findings is that while the creative people he studied seemed to *naturally* embrace opposing traits, it is possible for anyone to become more creative by simply understanding the dynamic. Deeming one trait acceptable and the other unacceptable is a learned behavior that can be unlearned. These are not, after all, moral qualities, but two sides of the same coin, two sides of the same human trait. They differ from our particular expression of "wisdom," which as Gardner found is necessarily lopsided, with strengths in two or three areas. "Understanding" is less fixed, in that mental dexterity can be developed and honed regardless of natural propensity toward one end of the spectrum of traits or the other.

When I was in a studio recording the audio version of my first book, the sound engineer took note of this dichotomy. He had not read the book before the session; he was hearing it for the first time as I was reading it aloud. But at about the midpoint, he stopped me to ask a question. How was it, he wondered, that someone who was so outwardly energetic, extroverted, and seemingly Type A (this was his assessment of me in the few hours we had spent together, and it wasn't altogether favorable) could have come to the conclusions in the book, which he saw as the fruit of deep introspection? It was a paradox to him; he didn't know how it was possible for me to have slowed down or sequestered myself enough to birth the insights in the book, which were children of a slower pace. This incongruity—my being *both/and* instead of *either/or*—confused him and even irritated him a little. If I was going to run deep, he wanted me to have still waters.

But more often the key is to hold two opposed ideas in the mind at the same time, as Fitzgerald suggested, and still function—and in terms of creativity, function better. When I made my vow to technical perfection, after Mrs. Davenport's jolting F, I was embracing caution only. Without the opposite pole of risk-taking, I was sealing the fate of my delicate little plant.

That's why displaying opposing traits doesn't create a split personality, but a complex one. And it offers another clue that creativity doesn't flow from one half of a split brain, but from both sides of an integrated one.

LEAPS

Given that understanding involves the ability to solve problems in a unique way—by finding common ground among dissimilar things, by putting two things together that are rarely joined in order to make something new—it makes perfect sense that having the full spectrum of human traits to work with and draw upon would enhance creativity. If the ability to make what scientists call "combinational leaps"—the bringing together of separate streams of thought—is the hallmark of creative thinking (and therefore biblical understanding), then leaps increase when you double the components.

The same logic applies to the brain itself: If using both sides of a human trait begets leaping, then so does using both sides of a human brain. Getting the two distinct sides of the brain, with their different and sometimes opposite functions, to work together is another example of *both/and* thinking, despite the popular belief that the right side alone houses creative inspiration. But my understanding of the right brain and its unique properties and the perilousness of its standing alone did not come from logic. The source of my insight was an experience both unexpected and dreamlike, like the discovery of my hidden room, with one variation: there was no dog with a special charge to speak, only a doctor who should have kept his mouth shut.

I'm not sure I knew anything was wrong at first; there may have been a hint here and there, like the time a visitor to our home made an interesting observation about our children. Our son, he said, was like a dog: he ran to the door, tongue wagging, eager to greet the newcomer. Our daughter, he noted, was more like a cat: she stole away as soon as she saw him coming. She was reluctant, or worse (for the visitor), disinterested. At the time I thought it was a harmless and fitting analogy. But as our children progressed beyond the toddler years, I realized people were not as accepting of my little cat-like daughter.

Then her behavior at a routine checkup wrested five small words from somewhere deep inside her pediatrician, which he disclosed in the most sophisticated medical jargon he could muster up: "I think Emily is off."

The word "off" hung between us as he droned on, recommending testing to confirm his suspicions, while I watched Emily playing, impervious to his slight. And maybe that was part of it; Emily *was* impervious. She had an uncanny ability to block out everything and everyone around her. "Does she have a hearing problem?" people would ask. "Does she talk at all?" If she wasn't tuning people out she was in the throes of a tantrum. A trivial event would set in motion an endless cycle of frustration and tears. Maybe he's right, I thought, glancing back at Emily in the rearview mirror on the way home. But then again, I had spent four years with this child and he had taken five minutes.

The next day I called the office to talk to the doctor again. I had done my homework, as he suspected I would, to learn more about the "pervasive developmental delay" label he had affixed to Emily. During the call, he seemed to backtrack a little, suggesting we wait six months before having Emily tested to see if she were just a "late bloomer." How casual he was with my little off child, throwing out terms like pervasive delay and late bloomer as if they were interchangeable.

RIGHT BRAIN, LEFT OUT

Emily didn't just march to the beat of a different drummer. She pranced and danced and flitted to that beat. Kinder people called her "spirited" and "dramatic." She wasn't always that way. She was a quiet, undemanding baby, who eased into the world just after Hurricane Emily hit the East Coast. On her first birthday, I wrote in her journal: "My dear Emily, I thought you were going to be a hurricane, but you turned out to be a breeze." And she was a breeze, ambling through the two's with little fanfare. It was when she turned three that I found my assessment had been premature. The tantrums began. There were times we had to drag her screaming from stores and restaurants. Doctors and dentists felt her knee reflex whether they wanted to or not. When something upset her, it would set in motion a series of overreactions that took on a life of their own.

Besides the behavioral glitches, there were also some developmental issues that worried us. Emily had difficulty learning to talk. I'm sure this contributed to the constant frustration that triggered her temper tantrums. She also had that uncanny ability to block out everything and everyone around her. That may have been her defense against an oversensitivity to noise, which she often said "screamed her ears." There had been whispers of concern before her pediatrician's pronouncement. I wasn't trying to deny reality, but I wasn't going to jump to conclusions either. After the visit to the pediatrician, my husband and I agreed to have Emily evaluated by a speech pathologist/audiologist. That's when we found out the technical term for Emily's problem. It's called: "She tunes people out on purpose."

Around that same time I began reading a story to Emily from Arnold Lobel's *Frog and Toad* series. In the story Toad plants a garden and then is impatient to see it grow. He plainly tells the seeds to grow, pacing among their rows for emphasis. When they do not comply, he presses his head to the ground and commands them to grow. Again the seeds lay, unlistening or unyielding, so Toad shouts louder for them to grow. I began to wonder if we have that same impatience with our children, when they are different, when they are off, when they don't progress at the same rate as other children. Emily had learned to walk and talk late; her behavior did seem more appropriate for a two-year-old than a four-year-old. Who was to say that this wasn't her appointed timetable? Perhaps in our frustration we were attempting to force her sprouts up too early. "These poor seeds are afraid to grow," suggests Frog to Toad, and then leaves him with this advice: "Let the sun shine on them, let the rain fall on them. Soon your seeds will start to grow."[4]

Frog's advice echoes Einstein's caution about holy curiosity: "for this delicate little plant, aside from stimulation, stands mainly in need of freedom." Where Frog says sunshine and rain are needed, Einstein says stimulation and freedom. Maybe what would quicken Emily was different from what caused other children to break through. What constituted her sunshine and rain? What would rouse and free her?

The answer to these questions came in the form of two books, passed along to me by a friend, written by Dr. Carla Hannaford, a neurobiologist: *Smart Moves: Why Learning Is Not All in Your Head* and *The Dominance Factor*. From these books we learned that Emily's learning profile is the one most likely to be labeled "learning disabled" in a traditional school setting; not necessarily because she is, but because schools tend to favor the logical left-brainers over the global right-brainers. Emily definitely leans right, as someone who focuses on the whole picture, someone whose learning is processed through movement and emotion. That's why she loves to dance. She would spend hours upon hours listening to everything from classical music to show tunes, making up elaborate dances that are pure emotional responses to what she hears. It's not exactly a gift that translates well into a structured classroom setting.

In addition to uncovering her learning style, we also determined to help Emily access her less dominant left brain, since logic, language, and linear processing are necessary in life, too. Simple movements known as Brain Gym® help to improve communication between the two sides of the brain.[5] The Brain Gym exercises (outlined in detail in Hannaford's *Smart Moves*) were developed by Dr. Paul Dennison, an educational therapist, in his attempts to help children and adults who had been labeled learning disabled. His clinical studies, begun in 1969, led him to the study of kinesiology, the science of body movement and its relationship to brain function. One of the most notable examples of the brain-body movement link is the connection researchers have found between crawling and reading. Crawling involves cross-lateral movements, in which both

4. Lobel, *Frog and Toad Together*, 20.

5. Brain Gym® is a registered trademark of Brain Gym® International/Educational Kinesiology Foundation. Brain Gym® movements used with permission from Paul and Gail Dennison.

sides of the body work together, evenly activating both sides of the brain. Since reading requires communication between the two hemispheres of the brain, children who missed the important crawling stage often struggle to read later on and may experience other learning difficulties.

Once we started these simple activities, we saw significant improvements in Emily's ability to communicate and to interact. No longer did she plead, "Mommy, I need more words." She had more self-control than we ever thought possible. She taught herself how to read and began to sit quietly through 4H. But she also retained her amazing "right brain" qualities; she still had a different air about her, she still liked to hold conversations with a silent listener, and she sometimes did the unexpected, like adding a not exactly choreographed flourish at the end of a dance recital.

I soon discovered that these movements—so crucial in unlocking Emily and so many other children with ADD, ADHD, autism, etc.—are also used widely in other learning ventures, under less dire circumstances. Many elementary-school teachers use the exercises throughout the course of the day, to focus the students and facilitate learning. I was even surprised to find that one of my children's reading CD-ROMs set the Brain Gym exercises to music, encouraging the child to do the exercises before any instruction takes place. But the exercises are not just for children: athletes (even weekend golfers) use them to enhance performance, musicians to play more passionately, and sales people to improve sales. But my most convincing argument for the exercises is Emily herself.

Soon after we began the Brain Gym exercises, I sent out my annual Christmas poem, a tongue-in-cheek tradition in which I recap the year's events to the cadence of "'Twas the Night Before Christmas." When it came time for me to recount the highlights of Emily's year, there was no room for irony:

> Emily found her voice, and its name is ballet
> With twists, twirls, and hops; an occasional plié.
> She's much like a flower that's found the right spot
> To unfold her petals, digging roots in the plot
> That's become her own special place in the sun
> The sprouting of Emily has only begun.

Perhaps "blossoming" would have been a prettier word. But Emily doesn't blossom. She sprouts. She exudes. She teems. And if that makes her an "off" child, then I'll gladly accept the consequences.

MENTAL GYMNASTICS

It was my son's birth that inspired me to break Smelly Nelly's curse and take back my delicate little plant, and it was my daughter's birth that taught me how to nurture it.

That's why I said my understanding of the right brain—and the perilousness of its standing alone—did not come from logic or a textbook or even my grad school training. It came from seeing what that peril looked like in the life of a four-year-old girl. What awakened her delicate little plant was a simple series of physical exercises that released the side of her brain that was being held hostage.

Most people, like Emily, show a preference for one brain hemisphere over the other; we are left-brained or right-brained just as we're left-handed or right-handed. While Emily's situation was more dramatic than most, everyone has had the experience of what it feels like to have a lopsided brain. Think of a stressful situation, like an exam or a job interview, where information you knew or studied is suddenly inaccessible. Under stress, the communication between the two sides of the brain is hindered, and only one hemisphere—the dominant one—is able to function efficiently.

What is temporary for us in times of stress was constant for Emily, and what was miraculous in Emily is remarkably helpful for anyone else. Because understanding, the second letter of the creative alphabet, is pliable, it can be adapted and strengthened regardless of natural propensity toward one hemisphere or the other. The lesson here is the same as with Csikszentmihalyi's findings about highly creative people: even if there is a natural leaning toward one end of the spectrum or the other—in this case, being right-brained or left-brained—the key is integration. The key is complexity over onesidedness.

Creativity, then, is a *whole* brain function that requires not only image, flow, and emotion from the right hemisphere, but technique and detail from the left hemisphere.[6] Facilitating that process is a simple series of movements designed to activate the neural networks in both hemispheres at the same time in order to build the "hardware" needed for learning, for thinking, for creativity.[7]

---

6. Hannaford, *Smart Moves*, 81.

7. Ibid., 130.

That's how I learned about the connection between movement and learning, or what Shaw would call activity and knowledge. That's how I knew to teach my college students the exercises. I discovered that thinking and learning and creativity flourish when movement is involved, when there is a connection made through movement so that mental gymnastics benefit from and are bolstered by, well, gymnastics. Mental dexterity can be enhanced through physical dexterity.

Of course, there is an element of dramatic irony in the fact that this experience with my daughter taught me that my least strong intelligence—the bodily-kinesthetic intelligence—is the key to creative thinking. And yet it shows how wisdom and understanding work together, so that an expression of one becomes the foundation of the other. Like the creative personality, like the brain itself, the components of holy curiosity work best when they work together.

THE BEST CREATIVE-THINKING EXERCISES I KNOW

It is the deep personal impact of my own experience with the Brain Gym movements coupled with the clear-cut scientific reasoning behind them that allow me to proclaim with confidence that they are the best creative-thinking exercises I know.

Whatever has been left undone, in terms of neural programming, can be made up for at any point in a person's life or development. Any person can use the exercises at any time for any number of purposes: to enhance creativity, to bolster performance in athletics and the arts, to increase workplace productivity, to alleviate stress.

While there are numerous Brain Gym movements, these four components comprise the routine I most often use with my children and college students, and do myself.

Water

The health benefits of water are well known, but Dr. Hannaford also calls it the "magic elixir" for learning and creativity. Keep hydrated throughout the day and *always* start the exercises by drinking water.

BRAIN BUTTONS®

To do this exercise, one hand is placed over the navel (to bring attention to the gravitational center of the body). The other hand is placed below the collar bone so that the fingers can gently rub the indentations between the first and second ribs directly under the collar bone, to the right and left of the sternum. This exercise increases blood and oxygen supply to the brain by stimulating blood flow through the carotid arteries and often renders a feeling of alertness, of "waking up." Coupled with water, I have found this exercise better at keeping me on my toes than a cup of coffee.

CROSS CRAWL®

This is a cross-lateral movement, just as regular crawling is. Stand and bring the right hand to the left knee and then left hand to the right knee, as if marching in place. This can also be done elbow to knee or backwards, with hands reaching back to touch alternating heels. The most important thing to remember is to do the Cross Crawl *very slowly*.

Boosting the argument for these kinds of slow, cross-lateral movements are recent studies that have found that while jogging is good exercise for the body, walking is better for the brain.[8] Walking is better because there is more oxygen left in the blood to reach the brain, which results in heightened attention and increased focus on specific tasks. Over the long term walking also helps to stave off strokes and mental decline.

Dr. Hannaford explains the science behind the Cross Crawl: "When done on a regular basis, more nerve networks form and myelinate in the corpus callosum, thus making communication between the two hemispheres faster and more integrated for high level reasoning."[9]

She also relates the life-transforming story of a sixteen-year-old boy named Todd who, though a sophomore in high school, still could not read. Because of his above-average height, he had also been recruited for the basketball team but was cumbersome on the court. His mother, a nurse, had learned about the Brain Gym exercises at a health conference. She immediately shared the exercises with Todd, especially focusing on the Cross Crawl, which they did together twice daily. Within six weeks, Todd was reading at grade level. Even his coordination on the basketball court improved. The elements he needed to read had been there for years, much like the components of Emily's speech, but he had not been

8. Bowman, "Walking Has Brain Benefits," para. 5.

9. Hannaford, *Smart Moves*, 119.

able to put them together. Todd has since graduated from college with a degree in biology.

HOOK-UPS®

To perform Hook-Ups, cross one ankle over the other (in any order, whatever is most comfortable). Then cross, clasp, and invert your hands. To do this, stretch your arms out in front of you, with the back of the hands together and the thumbs pointing down. Now lift one hand over the other, palms facing, and interlock the fingers. Then roll the locked hands straight down and in toward the body so they eventually rest on the chest with the elbows down. Close your eyes and breathe deeply for one minute (and up to five).

Not only does this exercise help to focus attention, it is an extremely effective way to self-soothe and reduce stress. Once, when her brother had especially exasperated her, Emily was heading into an angry spiral and then suddenly stopped herself, plopped on the kitchen floor, and rolled into hook-ups until she was calm enough to deal with her brother in a less physical way.

Dr. Hannaford says this is her most frequently used Brain Gym exercise, and I have often sneaked into a bathroom before a speaking event to calm and focus myself with this simple exercise. I also run through the entire routine each morning in the shower.

8

Letter Three: More Than Inspiration

Skill without imagination gives us many useful objects such as wicker-work picnic baskets. Imagination without skill gives us modern art.

Tom Stoppard

WHEN MUSIC LEGEND QUINCY Jones was asked the secret behind his prolific career, he thought for a moment and then answered: "Music visits me." That seems to have been the case for Mozart, too, who is famously recalled as having composed entire symphonies in his head before quill ever hit parchment. He left behind none of the endless drafts Beethoven pored over; it's possible the Muse preferred Wolfgang's rascality over Ludwig's bristles and favored the former with ease of process.

The word "music" is derived from the word Muse, but inspiration isn't solely symphonic. Think of all the poets who have invoked the Muse and produced similar masterpieces: Homer in Book I of *The Odyssey*, Dante in Canto II of *The Inferno*, and John Milton, who opens Book I of *Paradise Lost* by invoking the "Heavenly Muse," the Holy Spirit. Perhaps these visitations are all that's needed for creative inspiration.

Sometimes the credit goes not to the Muse but to the work itself, as with Michelangelo's contention that every block of stone has a statue inside that the sculptor must uncover (or carve down to the skin and stop). Writer Madeleine L'Engle likewise defers to the artistic endeavor itself: "I am convinced that each work of art, be it a great work of genius or something very small, has its own life, and it will come to the artist, the composer or the writer or the painter, and say, 'Here I am: compose me; or write me; or paint me'; and the job of the artist is to serve the work."[1] Another moving image of visitation, meant to be taken figuratively.

---

1. L'Engle, *Irrational Season*, 122.

What these inspired anecdotes fail to mention is that each artist had the *skill* required to serve the work, to release the image in the stone, to compose the cerebral symphonies. You can make the process sound simple, even ethereal, when you've got the goods. Taking the words literally leads to the false assumption that inspiration or imagination is enough. Einstein himself said imagination is more important than knowledge, but he wasn't talking about the biblical notion of knowledge, the one that when woven together with wisdom and understanding comprises the very holy curiosity he first described.

Still the idea that imagination is enough is far-reaching. One of my favorite classroom stories comes from another psychology professor who had commented on how a student's paper was written. The student's response: "That's just your opinion." The professor wasn't remarking on style or flow or even cohesive thought, just noting the objective mistakes: misspelled words, errant punctuation, incomplete sentences. But the student insisted that while the professor was entitled to her opinion, her opinion was wrong, and a new genre of expression was born: interpretive grammar.

It's that mindset, of self-expression at all costs or *no cost at all*, which may have elicited Tom Stoppard's scorn of modern art. Perhaps he was thinking of those artists who wore a black mood as if it were the mantle of creative personality. But it's impossible to distill creativity into a single factor, whether it's disposition or inspiration. Of course, inspiration is crucial too—not in a million years could a room full of monkeys reproduce the works of Shakespeare by thumping at typewriters—but it's a factor among factors; it cannot stand alone.

Biblical knowledge, which equates to technical know-how and expertise in Amabile's model, is equally as important as identifying your area of creativity and honing your ability to think creatively. There is a simple reason why attaining the practical skills to be creative is often dismissed: it is not instantaneous and it requires hard work. It requires using the bean-counting side of the brain. It requires understanding that there are objective mechanics of language and music and chiseling that need to be acquired in order for good writing, good scores, and good sculptures to happen.

That doesn't mean that you have to earn a degree in a certain area in order to be creative in it; there are dozens of ways to attain skills, to get knowledge. Some experts, including best-selling business author Daniel

Pink, predict an increase in self-teaching trends so that traditional four-year degrees will be replaced by apprenticeships (Shaw's activity as road to knowledge), distance learning, and what Pink calls "higher education just in time"—going to college to acquire particular *skills* instead of an entire diploma.[2]

But self-propelled learning can begin at any age. My son learned the basics of photography (an interest since he was four) by taking a correspondence course. I taught myself the first book in a piano-lessons series (having never tickled the ivories before) and then taught the lessons to my daughter. When she showed an aptitude and desire for it, I turned her over to a trained pianist.

For adults, community colleges have abundant offerings, including courses in everything from—with apologies to Tom Stoppard—basket weaving to modern art. You can even access free courses online from a number of top universities, complete with lectures on podcasts. A sample offering includes architecture (building in landscapes) at MIT, an introduction to robotics at Stanford, a film class at UC Berkeley, string theory at Harvard, poetry at Yale, and entrepreneurship at Carnegie Mellon.

Once you understand your area of creativity, which of the multiple intelligences are most strongly yours, you need only decide in what ways to explore them. For example, if a person whose strength is linguistic chooses to explore writing, is it poetry or blogging? If the same person chooses to explore speaking, is it Toastmasters or foreign languages? Once decided, the focus is on attaining the skills necessary to be truly creative in that area.

Of course, the same advice works both ways: skill alone is not enough. Skill alone is what I had when I pledged myself to technical perfection in order to wrest an A from Mrs. Davenport. And although I disagree with Tom Stoppard that picnic baskets can't be inspired, the pith of his statement is true: holy curiosity has components that have to work in tandem in order for creativity to flourish.

To uncover exactly *how* these components work in tandem becomes my next task, the next image to be released from the stone. I know how the process of creativity works scientifically, but not with the creative letters of God's alphabet.

So I return to the description of Wisdom's house, and continue chiseling the passage, until I reach the skin.

2. Pink, *Free Agent Nation*, 256.

GREAT WORLD, LITTLE WORLD

If the framing of Wisdom's house is described with the same language as the creation of the world, if her house is a mirror held up to the first act of creation, then it must contain a clue as to the divine pattern of creative acts.

So I search the parallel passages again—the macrocosm and microcosm of creativity in Proverbs 3 and 24—and find there is one more repetition I had missed. Besides the duplication of wisdom, understanding, and knowledge, there is another word—this time a word of action—that appears in both:

- The heavens are *set* in place, in the creation of the world (3:19),

and

- the house is *set* on a firm foundation, in the creation of Wisdom's holy space (24:3).

The Hebrew root *kwn* is the same in both passages and is translated *set* or *established*. In general, it means to bring something into existence. But specifically, it evokes the conviction that the something brought into existence is beyond dispute, like the incontrovertible proof in a court case.

The idea of bringing something into incontrovertible existence is strikingly similar to the first definition of creativity I offered, in the very first chapter: For creativity to happen, something within you must be brought to life in something outside of you. That's exactly the meaning behind this concept of *setting* or *establishing*.

Although the Hebrew root and its derivatives occur 288 times in the Old Testament, it is only in these *two* passages that it occurs in combination with wisdom, understanding, and knowledge. The four words together, then, occur only twice in the entire reach of the Hebrew Scriptures, in these two places, the "great world" and "little world" of God's creative process.

When I follow the path of this word more closely—to find how it is used and in what context—a pattern emerges: a well-defined progression of steps by which the creative process is accomplished, the means by which a particular "something" is brought into existence. The word then not only reflects a modern-day definition of creativity but blazes an ancient trail to get there.

When I place these steps side by side with the stages of the creative process I've already been teaching, I can match them nearly word for word. How can it be that all of these elements are fixed in a single term that never would have surfaced in a search, even an exhaustive one, of the concept of "creating" or "creativity" in the Bible? Instead the word—and the age-old pattern contained within it—has been embedded, like fine furniture and beautiful draperies, in Wisdom's house.

The steps enfolded in the root *kwn* are culled from its use throughout the Old Testament and fall into several distinct stages.[3] The first stage involves the task of making or getting ready, when the idea of what is to be brought to life is forming but has not clearly taken shape. "Formation without firmness" is how one biblical scholar defines it. Charles Dickens is a little more artful: "An idea, like a ghost . . . must be spoken to a little before it will explain itself."[4] This phase is much like what social scientists call the *preparation stage* of the creative process.

In fact, one of the most important elements of the preparation stage is *knowledge*, the practical skills necessary for a particular area of creativity. So the last letter in the creative alphabet, which is also the third component in Amabile's model, becomes a key to the first stage in the process by which these same letters or components are combined.

Just as one aspect of wisdom became the foundation of understanding, so now knowledge leads the process by which all three are combined.

THE ARCHITECT

Emerson, who has already proven he knows Wisdom's various expressions well, constructed a poem about a house that sounds much like hers. In it he states that the Muse can out-build any architect, for:

> She is skilful to select
> Materials for her plan.[5]

---

3. Zodhiates, *Hebrew-Greek*, 1600.

4. Grothe, *I Never Metaphor I Didn't Like*, 294.

5. Emerson, "The House," 98.

It's interesting that he chose the word "skillful," which is an apt synonym for knowledge, the final letter in our alphabet of three. But that's only one of the "materials" needed; wisdom and understanding must also be there. But even materials are not enough; there needs to be a "plan," a blueprint for the creative process.

Now I know that *both* the materials *and* the plan have been there all along, hidden in this passage of Scripture. They have been built into the description of Wisdom's house, a house I never would have found had not my dream been cast as its shadow. But it was cast and is now unraveled, so that its purpose is made clear: While Wisdom's house is a mirror image of creation, the scientific theories of creativity are mirror images of Wisdom's house.

And it is the Architect of that house who can out-build any Muse.

PART THREE

Following the Pattern

9

Levels One and Two:
Blue Prints and Green Indigestion

Spontaneity comes after skill, not before.

Mason Cooley

Picasso called it green indigestion. His idea was to go for a stroll through the forest, perhaps instinctively aware that the movement itself was kindling his creative spark, with the goal to take in the most abundant color it offered: green. Once fully sated, and with a case of "green indigestion," he returned home and disgorged the color onto his canvas: a verdant masterpiece. Dickens had likened this initial stage of the creative process to a wispy ghost, but Picasso made it much more tangible, or as tangible as vomiting color can be.

Often a creative act is perceived as spontaneous overflow, but it is surprising how prepared you have to be in order to be spontaneous. You can't spill green unless you first fill green. That's the main purpose of the first stage of the creative process.

I taught this stage in my classes, but that was before I discovered that the entire body of creativity research had been tucked inside these four small words penned centuries ago. Now that I had uncovered the parallels to wisdom, understanding, and knowledge, I wanted to explore the process—both the scientific path and the ancient trail—by which creative elements are combined. What is the blueprint for rearranging the something of God?

Those who have studied the cycle of creativity have found that the creative process can typically be broken down into five stages or steps. This corresponds to the number of stages that unfolds biblically when something is brought into incontrovertible existence, although the biblical process exposes an unexpected layer that its scientific counterpart does not. Still, the conclusion is the same: While there were two steps involved in the creation of man (fashioning and then breathing life into), there are five steps involved when man himself creates.

That man is allowed to create is a gift; that it takes him longer is a gentle reminder from whence the gift comes.

STEP ONE: BE PREPARED

Both Dickens and Picasso were right about this first stage in the creative process; there is a fuzziness to it, but there is also some concrete work to be done. When referring to this beginning stage, the root *kwn* is often translated "fashioning" and is much like the molding and shaping of the clay Adam. It fits Dickens's spectral depiction, as I mentioned before, when the something being brought into existence is forming but not firm. Even so, there are some practical ways to coax the ghost into explaining itself.

This stage is often called the preparation stage, and how you prepare is important. One way is to fill yourself up, like Picasso did, so that there *can be* something inside of you to be brought to life outside of you. "The painter passes through states of fullness and emptying," Picasso told a colleague in explaining what he meant by green indigestion. "That is the whole secret of art . . . The painter paints as if in urgent need to discharge himself of his sensations and his visions."[1] But how does the painter or any other artisan arrive at these sensations and visions? The key to fullness is to have an open mind, to be open to anything and everything that's even loosely related to your endeavor. Just as embracing both ends of the spectrum enhances the creative personality, so being open to as many ideas from as many different sources as possible enhances the creative process. In both cases, the outcome is the same: you have multiplied the components with which to make combinational leaps, those unique and unlikely pairings that are the hallmark of creative thinking.

The ability to embrace the full repertoire of human traits, then, has a corollary that moves beyond the area of personality and into the area of attention. A recent study revealed that the brains of creative people "filter" less than their peers; that is, they are more open to the information, input, and stimuli constantly streaming in from their environments. They have open minds, literally. There is a positive side to this filtering,

---

1. Ghiselin, *Creative Process*, 51.

called latent inhibition, and that is to prevent sensory overload (being too open to incoming stimuli wouldn't be a good idea when driving a car or performing brain surgery, for example). Typically what people filter is what is perceived to be irrelevant to their needs.

But those who tested high on creativity also tested low on latent inhibition, indicating that creative people are able to take in *more* sensory data *without* feeling overloaded or deeming it irrelevant. Again, it's a matter of simple mathematics; the more bits and pieces you take in, the greater the chance those bits and pieces will align themselves in a novel way.[2]

Latent inhibition is an automatic biological response and happens unconsciously, in much the same way creative people by nature draw from both ends of the spectrum. But just as we can boost the creativeness of our personalities by displaying opposing traits, we can also consciously determine to filter out less of our rich environment.

"The normal person," one of the study's researchers concludes, "classifies an object, and then forgets about it, even though that object is much more complex and interesting than he or she thinks. The creative person, by contrast, is always open to new possibilities."[3]

Writer Frederick Buechner offers a spiritual interpretation of this same idea: "We are all of us more mystics than we believe or choose to believe . . . We have seen more than we let on, even to ourselves. Through some moment of beauty or pain, some sudden turning of our lives, we catch glimmers at least of what the saints are blinded by; only then, unlike the saints, we tend to go on as though nothing has happened."[4]

We can take both the researcher's scientific findings and the writer's spiritual eloquence to heart when seeking to become more creative: al-

---

2. There is a second group of people who have also tested low on latent inhibition in past studies: those who suffer from mental illness. While they share this capacity with the creative group, they differ in that taking in more stimuli *does* lead to feeling overloaded and disoriented. (Some researchers believe the difference is that those who struggle with mental illness have difficulty determining whether the stimuli are coming from within themselves or outside of themselves.) The conclusion of the study is that low levels of latent inhibition—being more open to incoming stimuli—might predispose some individuals to mental illness and others to creative achievement. Perhaps this accounts for the long-standing but misguided link forged between creativity and mental illness; both can follow from this biological ability to filter less stimuli but with very different outcomes.

3. "Biological Basis for Creativity Linked to Mental Illness," para. 3.

4. Buechner, *A Room Called Remember*, 152–53.

ways be open to new possibilities, go on as though something has happened. That's the first and most important step as you begin the creative process.

An important aspect of latent inhibition, the protective factor, is that it screens out what is perceived to be irrelevant in order to prevent overload. But when being creative, especially in the beginning stage, almost everything *is* relevant. This idea goes against the grain of thinking in almost any field, at least since we've moved away from being Renaissance men and toward being specialists. We are a culture trained to specialize, to narrow our focus to become saturated in one field only. By doing so, we make a *conscious* decision to filter out important stimuli and remain open only to those ideas or elements that fit neatly into a particular specialty. A few of the business majors who were required to take my creativity course complained that there was too much psychology in it; they were equally dismayed when I imported literature (from children's books to Virginia Woolf) into the course material. They scratched their heads when we watched movie clips and when I invited a seasoned guitarist to play for them. How were those disciplines going to help them succeed in business? They wanted numbers and strategies, like the rest of their business classes.

But many business leaders understand that specializing in a single field, trying to become an expert in one discipline, often lessens the ability to be creative in that field. "Experts" exclude the rich resources outside of their field; they have only similar things to combine, and there are no leaps made when the elements are alike. That doesn't negate getting to know a field as well as possible—spontaneity comes after skill after all—but it does discourage limiting input to that field alone. An antonym for "specialize" is "broaden," and broadening is the goal of the preparation stage.

A PLACE FOR FRUSTRATION

There is one more thing to be "open" to during the preparation stage: frustration. Because creativity is often viewed as something that flows from the artist effortlessly, most people think they're doing it wrong if there is frustration involved. Or they give up too soon if there's an obstacle. Recently I saw an image of a writer on a television program. He sat comfortably in the dark with nothing but the light from his laptop; there were no notes, no piles of research at his elbow, nothing but his brain and his word processor, both humming contentedly. But there is much room for discontent when creating. Even Picasso's spilling green was only a masterpiece because he had tried and failed, struggled with the images on his canvas, slogged through the intense training he needed as a painter before he ever took the stroll through the forest. There was nothing spontaneous and effortless about his *skill*; that was the result of many years of training at the hands of his father, an art professor who insisted on technique both traditional and academic. Picasso needed those skills even if—especially if—he was going to use them in a way they had never been used before, taking them apart and reassembling them at random angles as he did his subjects. That's why the biblical idea of knowledge, the painstaking process of acquiring the skills to be creative, is not only part of the preparation stage but part of what makes the stage frustrating.

Although one of the most overlooked components of creativity, frustration is not only common but necessary to successfully move through this and other stages in the creative process. It should be embraced, and while it's not a polar trait on one side of the spectrum the way playfulness and discipline are, it is an emotion that is usually labeled "bad" and shouldn't be. I often refer to this stage as grappling because there's disquiet and a sense of not being able to pin down what you want to say or do or think or create; the ghost hasn't yet taken shape so it is hard to grasp.

Anticipating and accepting frustration becomes an essential step to creative breakthrough. I have come to distrust my own creative aspirations if there is little frustration involved, and while I don't agree with George Orwell that writing a book is like suffering through a painful illness, I do think that anyone who hums contentedly through the creative process is more actor than artist.

STEP TWO: INCUBATE

When I was in the beginning stages of writing my first book, I was waylaid by a real illness, not the pretend illness Orwell compared book-writing to. For three days I lay in bed, forced to sleep off a persistent sinus infection. When I did come to, in brief moments of consciousness,

I lamented how behind I was in my work. There was a deadline looming but I wasn't even well enough to sit up much less work in bed.

My body had fought the imposed passivity and lost. But fortunately the moratorium came after months of "filling green," months of research and exploration and being open to any and all ideas and resources. When I finally awoke from three days of what felt like poisoned-apple-induced stupor, there it was, like a rescuing prince—the complete outline of the book—perfectly constructed in my head.

When the publisher received the manuscript many months later, the most striking thing he said was this: "We knew the writing would be top-notch but we've all agreed the real genius of the book lies in its structure. It is inspired." Yes, inspired by three days in a near-coma.

Of course, the reason inspiration struck is that I had filled green, *but* there was a major step in between filling and spilling that assured everything spilled into the right place. That step is called incubation.

Just as with a bird sitting on a clutch of eggs, there are two components that define creative incubation: stillness and patience. But being still and being patient are often viewed as being *passive*, another trait on the spectrum that we avoid because we view it as "bad." (I admit that I was a reluctant visitor to this end of the spectrum.) We equate passivity with laziness, and when the passivity is required, it is easy to become discouraged. Feelings of stagnation can cause us to despair.

One of the images I call to mind during times of needful inertia is drawn from spiritual writer Thomas Moore, in which he likens the captivity of stillness to Jonah being swallowed by the whale: "Imagine that your dark mood, or the external source of your suffering, is a large, living container in which you are held captive. But this container is moving, getting somewhere, taking you to where you need to go . . . Sometimes in your darkness you may sense that something is *incubating* in you."[5]

My whale for those three days was my sickbed, and while I perceived myself anchored by it, I was being taken to where I needed to go, to a breakthrough that had to travel through stillness and patience to be reached. "You are going somewhere, even though there are no external signs of progress," reassures Moore.

During Jonah's misadventure he too spends three days and nights confined, in much less amiable surroundings than mine, all the while creating his own sort of indigestion. At last the whale vomits him onto

5. Moore, *Dark Nights*, 4. Italics added.

dry ground. He is delivered, figuratively and literally, having been rescued from a watery death, and set down in a place that is one step closer to fulfilling his call to preach to the Ninevites. Despite Jonah's own mistakes (and running from God is a big one), the whale became his provision—and transport. Such are times of imposed passivity in our own lives.

Even though Moore is addressing despair in particular, he calls what is happening during this kind of experience "creative," and it is, because it's a vivid picture of the *activity in inactivity* that occurs during the incubation stage.

My incubation had been involuntary and unplanned, but I have since learned to embrace the passive nurturing required of this stage. I had stumbled upon a natural rhythm in the creative process, a step that social scientists have confirmed again and again as the one best suited to follow intense preparation. It is a time to let simmer, just below the threshold of consciousness, all the information having an open mind has let in.

While I slept my mind was busy assimilating the information, re-arranging bits and pieces and making connections I was unaware of. But incubation doesn't require *complete* inactivity; you don't have to be as immobilized as I was to simply refrain from actively working on a creative solution. Many people have had breakthroughs like mine while taking a shower or driving a car. Isaac Newton was meandering through a garden, his body moving and mind wandering, when he envisioned the now proverbial apple falling from a tree and it occurred to him that the gravity that made the apple fall to the ground may also hold the moon in its orbit. Another scientist, a chemist, discovered the structure of the benzene molecule not in a laboratory but at the end of long day when he sat simply gazing into a fire. The dancing flames gave him the image he needed for a major breakthrough in organic chemistry.

Incubation works best at the midpoint between frenetic activity and near-coma; the key is to be in a state of *relaxed receptivity*. The mind is not wide open as it is during the preparation stage but closes its gates a bit to continue the creative process sans sights and sounds. It is a time free of noise and distraction, to simply let thoughts wend their way above the din of television, computers, cell phones, car radios—the constant noise that daily bombards us. There are no epiphanies at rock concerts.

So I'll take the opportunity to add to the symptomology of Picasso's colorful analogy, and say thus far the stages of creativity follow this or-der: Fill, *keep still*, then spill.

10

Levels Three and Four: Beyond "Aha!"

In the case of the creative mind, it seems to me, the intellect has with-drawn its watchers from the gates, and the ideas rush in pell-mell, and only then does it review and inspect the multitude.

Friedrich von Schiller

I HAD LIKENED MY three-day sleep to a stupor induced by poison apple, but in some versions of the fairy tale what saves the damsel in distress is not the kiss of a rescuing prince but a bumpy ride that dislodges the bit of poisoned apple stuck in her throat. As grateful as I was to be roused from my own sleep of death with an antidote to my poison, which in this case was not an apple but a book that was yet wispy ghost, there was one problem. The perfectly constructed book outline was still in my head. I needed a way to dislodge it.

When I attempted to transfer the outline from head to paper (propping up the specter with its first skeleton), it didn't come out with Roman numerals attached. It didn't line up between the perfect margins Mrs. Davenport insisted upon. Instead, it spilled onto poster board in a spiral of images and arrows that looked more like a treasure map than a book outline.

I was using a process called mind-mapping, a tool designed to help crack the egg after incubation, to organize ideas in a way that is natural to the brain. Mind-mapping is not new (there are some indications it's been around in some form since at least the third century AD), but it has enjoyed a resurgence of interest since author and educational consultant Tony Buzan modernized the concept—too late for my graduate-school training. I discovered and taught myself the technique during my first semester as a psychology professor at the university.

The mind map follows an associative rather than linear pattern, making use of the interconnections that are the hallmark of creative thinking. It is spillage—the process of emptying—but not in an I, II, III, or A, B, C sort of way. Instead you start with a blank slate and a central image or theme.

There are different ways to approach mind-mapping, but these are a few basics that made my head-to-paper transfer possible:

- Start with a blank sheet of paper—or something bigger if you can get it, such as poster board—and turn it horizontally.[1]

- In the center, print a word or phrase to represent your subject matter. You can even draw a picture. Circle the word or image to reinforce its centrality. Printing is also recommended over cursive writing for easier readability and because block letters make a stronger mental impression.

- In the open spaces of the page, write down as quickly as possible key words (not phrases) associated with the central word.

- Do not edit at this stage, but write down everything that comes to mind.

- Use lines to connect the key words to the central word or image. (Ideally the lines should be thicker at the point they intersect with the central word or image and then gradually get thinner as they attach to the key words, as if radiating from the center.)

- Draw additional branches out from the key words as the key words spur subcategories. Put each key word on top of its own line or branch, as well as the subcategories that come to mind.

- Also recommended is the use of *color* (typically three or more colors) and *images* whenever possible to enhance and represent the key words.

- Use arrows to link key words and images with one another. The key to this process is the natural association that happens as the words and images spill out. Catch these associations and connect them with arrows.

---

1. Loosely adapted from Michalko, *Cracking Creativity*, 58–59.

- Revise as needed, but during the "spilling" phase of mind-mapping, resist the urge to make changes. Instead use this opportunity to "empty" only, as Picasso said, and refine later.

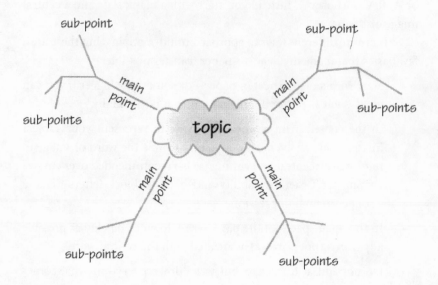

Mind-map image. © The Open University.
Reproduced by kind permission.

FREE FLOW

In its initial stages, mind-mapping mirrors the practice of free association, a technique used in the talking therapies. It coaxes spontaneous response without censorship in order to mine the riches of incubation, the stuff lying just beneath the reach of conscious thought. Like free association, mind-mapping works because it utilizes the brain's natural ability to combine and connect, to make intuitive leaps that don't follow a straight path. In the creative process, mind-mapping evokes the spontaneity that springs from a prepared mind.

But if mind-mapping works because it sidesteps the linear pattern of an A-B-C outline, why are the stages of the creative process neatly stacked one on top of the other? Where is the free flow in the process itself? The truth is that the creative process, whether defined scientifically or spiritually, is rarely so fixed. It has the fluidity of a cascade not the discreteness of a stepladder, with stages that can be repeated indefinitely, interrupted by other stages, and vary in length from minutes to years.

While I had spent many months preparing, three days incubating, and a few hours mind-mapping, I had not emerged from the first two stages of the creative process for the last time, not in this particular project or any other. Preparation would continue, incubation would continue, and many times would I pass through and return to the next stage in the creative process: insight.

My mind map had served as a link between two stages, building a bridge from the passive part of incubation to the active "aha" of insight. It dislodged my gestated thoughts, allowing them to arrange and rearrange themselves on paper and giving them a substance and visibility that made the insights of the next stage possible. The two phases fused so that it was impossible to tell where one began and the other ended.

The steps in the creative process are more descriptive than directive. They can't be interpreted too literally; in the same way no one really believes there are 1.86 children in the average American family. Children can't be fractionalized, nor should the process that brings forth the offspring of a creative mind.

"AHA!" MOMENTS

Insight is the next step in the creative process, the time for great epiphanies, of "aha" moments and cries of "Eureka!" It's the stage most people are referring to when they speak of visitations from the Muse. Once I had my incubated ideas and images on paper, I was quickly able to make connections between them, translating them into the insights that formed the core of the book. Apart from Muse-like inspiration, that is *technically* what insight is: it is what occurs, in terms of learning theory, when you are able to connect things in a way that helps you solve new problems or create new products. As I began to write the book itself, I continually looked to my map for direction (just like a real map) and while I was not beholden to it, in the end it proved so reflective of the soul of the book that I rarely veered from its course. The cascading nature of the creative process is especially evident here because insight is not as much a separate stage as it is the overflow of the two previous stages. It's a burst of light, a glorious harvest, a surprise uprising and then the hard work begins again.

This was not the first time I had drawn insight from a mind map (or onto a mind map). The technique is aptly named because it can point you in the right direction, but what if the path has already been blazed?

One day I decided to use mind-mapping *retroactively*, not to unearth but to understand. And while the mind map of my book had coaxed a reluctant ghost into explaining itself, this map offered evidence of a much greater Spirit already at work.

One Monday afternoon I was sitting at the kitchen table in the home of my son's guitar teacher, listening as their lesson progressed in the next room, grateful when it was punctuated by sublime duets. Buoyed by the music, like the Old Testament prophets whose utterances were evoked by song, I turned my blank sheet of paper sideways, took pencil in hand, and began to sketch out my map. I wasn't looking for a springboard from incubation; instead I was looking back and recording what had already been.

I'm not sure where I got the idea. I had never read about using a mind map in this way. But I did know the technique facilitated connections, and I was curious if any connections would surface between the various things I had done professionally since I finished graduate school. It may have been an exercise in futility because up to that point my career path was more of a ramble, and my hunch was that my being all over the map professionally would show itself, well, all over the map.

When my father was in hospice, and my sisters and I were trying to determine his level of awareness, we would ask him endless questions about what year it was or who the current president was. Before the merciful nurses were able to stop us, I got in one final question: "Dad, what do I do for a living?"

At the time I had taken a break from teaching to write my first book, and of course he had been aware of those changes, but this is how he answered: "Well, you're a wife and mother first. You consider those two things your most important jobs." He was quiet a moment before adding, "Then you do whatever else that comes along that interests you."

He was right, of course, in the way that dying people often are, when their words matter most. Never had I heard my adult life summed up quite so succinctly.

What I discovered, though, when I started to map out my professional steps was that the haphazardness of my "interests" had been a misperception. I was surprised by the arrows that linked this project to that, by how each step uniquely prepared me for the next, how my creative gifts were stirred up and strengthened and stretched, and how decisions unrelated to career or creative expression, except to limit them in some ways (such as the decision to educate my kids at home), were just as important in equipping me for the next position as were my education and work experience.

My passage from one place to another was rarely logical; the pass-key from one opportunity to the next never the obvious one. My first invitations to speak at professional seminars, for example, had nothing to do with my English degree but flowed from my experiences home-schooling my children. Those speaking opportunities piqued my interest in classroom teaching, which led to my adjunct position at the university, which brought me back to my original career path in psychology, which had been sidetracked by eight years as a television writer. But the first class I taught at the university was less connected to my graduate degree in psychology than to my experience writing training scripts for a video production company. Those scripts and the courses designed around them featured all the foundational material for organizational behavior, the first course I taught at the university. And I got the script-writing job based on my experience writing for TV, which, of course, I was offered while hunting for a job in psychology. Even the material I used in the second course that I developed for the university—my creativity course—was gathered in large part from my experiences with my daughter Emily and the quest she set me on to embrace the differences in creative expression. All the areas of creativity unearthed by the inventory I took when I first started teaching—linguistic, logical, and intrapersonal—had been carefully interwoven into opportunities before I fully understood that these were the ways Wisdom expressed herself through me.

So the course my father had identified, of my being a wife and mother first, and then an interest-follower, spilled onto the page into what looked like a perfectly orchestrated career path. But I had done none of the orchestrating.

One of my former students, who had taken my creativity class several years ago, called the university the other day and asked for me. The office manager of the psychology department told him I wasn't teaching there anymore. "Well, where is she teaching then?" he asked. She told him I wasn't teaching anywhere at the moment, but was writing full time. His note arrived in my inbox the next day: "I never imagined you would leave the classroom."

There's an aspect of the creative life that is less map and more path. There is a template to the creative process anyone can follow, but the path is something more personal.

That's what I learned from the map I sketched at the kitchen table during my son's guitar lesson. Of course, I wasn't the first to come to this conclusion. "The steps of a man are established by the LORD," declared the psalmist David (Ps 37:23a, NASB). But there is more to my and David's "aha" moments than I first realize. The word "established" is familiar to me by now, and when I look up the verse in the original language I discover it is the same Hebrew word found in Prov 3 and 24, in the passages unveiling the "great world" and "little world" of God's creative process. It is the same word that has been embedded in Wisdom's house, unfolding the pattern of the creative process, the very pattern I followed to bring forth this insight. The word doesn't just "establish" the divine pattern of creative acts, but here discloses that there is something *else* established by God, something *else* that is brought into incontrovertible existence: our steps.

Until now, the models of creativity have been parallel in that when the biblical process of bringing something into incontrovertible existence is followed through Scripture, it goes through the same initial stages as its scientific equivalent.

But here the two models diverge for a moment to reveal an unexpected layer: God not only sets in order the steps of the creative process, but determines the path we take as we carry them out. The path itself is a creative act of God.

That's why I left the open classroom of a professor to live the cocooned life of a writer, exchanging for a time students for readers, writing words instead of speaking them. Because it was not interests I had been following after all.

INSPECTING THE MULTITUDE

There is a natural ebb and flow to the creative process that is much like the back and forth of the creative personality, from playful to disciplined, from imaginative to realistic, from highly energetic to calmly at rest. The hard work of preparation is followed by the relaxed receptivity of incubation, which then binds up and gathers in the sheaves of insight. But once the harvest is in, once the "ideas rush in pell-mell," it is time, as von Schiller asserted in the opening quote, to "review and inspect the multitude."

That's the task of the next stage of the creative process, evaluation. Reviewing and inspecting the multitude means determining whether the insights that arise from incubation are novel enough to pursue. After the initial euphoria of inception we ask, are the insights still viable? Can they live on their own? Once the ghost explains itself, is what he has to say worth putting flesh on? This stage can cause emotional upheaval that serves the same clarifying purpose frustration does. Feelings of insecurity surface as each insight is weighed in the balance. Will it be found wanting? When it is, an "aha" moment can quickly dissolve into an "oh, no" moment.

I read a newspaper article recently about a pile of old paintings found in the back of the janitor's closet in a small-town church in Minnesota. Most were cheap reproductions but among them one painting held promise. When the pastor of the church sought the advice of an art institute to preserve the piece, it was discovered that the painting was the work of Ary Scheffer, a celebrated Romantic painter who worked in Paris the first half of the nineteenth century. Although Scheffer painted the portraits of such luminaries as Chopin and Liszt, the subject of this painting was more luminous still: Christ in his role as comforter to the brokenhearted. When appraised, "Christus Consolator" was valued at $35,000, and though once buried deep like the talent in the parable, it is now on proud display at the Minneapolis Institute of Arts. Art experts and church members alike found it difficult to believe that a piece so valuable aesthetically and important historically—it was one of the most popular religious images in the Western world in the mid-1900s—had languished for decades in a broom closet among cheap imitations and works of little or no value. (Sometimes Wisdom hides hymns in five hundred-year-old paintings, and sometimes she just hides the paintings.)

The evaluation stage follows a similar course as this fortuitous closet-cleaning: Not all insights are *original*. Some are *reproductions*, some are posers, and others are not worth keeping because they have no real value. The task of evaluation—the centerpiece of the word is *value*—

is to determine which insight belongs in which pile, what goes to Goodwill and what goes to the Guggenheim.

But the decisions shouldn't be made too hastily. While mind-mapping is done quickly and without censoring, evaluation is done slowly and deliberately. Imagine if the pastor had judged all the paintings based on the first one he came to? He would have missed out on the one treasure hidden beneath the others. "In every work of genius," Emerson observed, "we recognize our own rejected thoughts."[2] In order to prevent rejecting the wrong thoughts, creativity experts warn against the voice of judgment, the inner voice of criticism that silences our creative impulses. It's also important to be discriminating when sharing new and still-fragile insights with others; as often as not the voice of judgment can sound outside of us.

There is, of course, a counter to a voice that judges too harshly and that is a voice that commends too quickly. Part of this stage, part of what constitutes the scales upon which each insight is weighed, is a working knowledge of the field itself. This includes not only the practical skills associated with a field but a grasp of the internalized opinion of the field (what other members of the field expect). The more knowledge you have of your area of creativity, the better equipped you are to avoid either overestimating or underestimating the true value of your insights.

What may have surprised the art experts who identified Scheffer's painting is that no one really expects to find treasure in a church closet—or any other place in a church, especially not these days. Perhaps that says something about modern religious art, or more pointedly, art by the modern religious. Leading Bible scholar N. T. Wright is more temperate: "The church doesn't have a monopoly on kitsch or sentimentalism, but if you want to find it, the church may well be the easiest place to start."[3] But why is that the case?

In the biblical pattern of creativity, the evaluation stage carries the idea of *fixing in place*, with the intention that the placement be permanent. During the creation account, for example, the heavens are first *prepared* and then *fixed* in place (establishing the order of all subsequent

2. Emerson, *Self-Reliance*, 19.

3. Wright, *Surprised by Hope*, 223.

creative acts). What gives this stage its sense of permanence in our creative endeavors, besides the careful eye of evaluation, is knowing whether or not we are following God's path—not a general template but a specific path. And if we are, then that is the source of our confidence, that is what assuages the insecurity that plagues this stage. So assured, shouldn't we expect more of ourselves—as those armed with wisdom, knowledge, and understanding; as those following God's own divine design of creativity; as those confident in the knowledge that our steps are not random but ordered? Shouldn't we then be capable of *original* works that eschew janitor's closets in favor of art galleries, that line bookshelves, that fill concert halls, that revolutionize industry, that change lives?

Scheffer thought so, as did Vincent Van Gogh, who as a young teacher and preacher beseeched his brother to purchase a copy of "Christus Consolator" and send it to him, so that its message would serve as inspiration to his own emerging artistic ability. Van Gogh wrote a note of thanks to his brother for the copy of Scheffer's painting, along with a word of encouragement: God can always be trusted to lead us on the right path. While I knew that was true in general, I now know it's especially true when I create. And that, dear Vincent, is an insight worth keeping.

11

Levels Five and More:
Bringing What's Inside You
to Life Outside of You

The palette and the easel, my darling play-mates once,
must be my sober toil-fellows now.

Anne Brontë

THE EARLIEST STAGES OF the creative process are the most fluid, and that's not a figurative image only. There is a gathering in, a filling up, and a spilling out so that the biblical counter to Picasso's gastrointestinal analogy is a beautiful picture of how God "establishes" rain for the earth (Ps 147:8) by the same method he has established for us to create: the moisture is gathered up into clouds and once sated they burst, replenishing the earth and allowing the cycle to begin again. The creative process follows the natural course of rainmaking (filling and spilling) up to this point but becomes less cyclical and pliable during evaluation, in readiness for the final stage, when what is inside of you is brought to life outside of you.

That final stage is called elaboration. Elaboration is what won out when Edison decided to fractionalize creative genius, divvying it up into the now proverbial 1 percent inspiration and 99 percent perspiration—another fluid analogy. Elaboration is sometimes called translation, because the evaluated insight is translated into something solid and permanent. It is the hardest work of the hard work of creativity, when darling play-mates become sober toil-fellows, but it's also the most rewarding.

During the last stage of the creative process there is a return to the first stage; elaboration calls for the same open-mindedness as preparation. It is time again to be open to ideas and input, and not just from external stimuli. It is equally important to pay attention to what's going on inside, to gauge your emotional reaction to how efforts are progressing and whether goals are being met. Insights are no longer fragile and need not be protected; they have been tested (through evaluation) and found gold, and it is time to let others in and to seek out advice, especially from those already established in your field of creativity.

Vincent van Gogh, in one of the many letters to his brother Theo that now provide a window to his inner life, summed up the creative process this way: "The rough draught turns into a sketch, and the sketch into a painting through the serious work done on it, through the elaboration of the original vague idea and through the consolidation of the first fleeting and passing thought."[1] Succinctly he outlines the stages of creativity from the wispy ghost of a "vague idea" to the "serious work" of elaboration, from that which is fleeting to that which is made solid.

And making solid—through elaboration—is where the process ends, at least in the scientific model of creativity. The painting is hung, the poem recited, the equation solved, the dance performed, the flowers blossom. As lovely and as important as each of these accomplishments is, the spiritual counterpart finds it necessary to carry out the process one step further.

No one came to appreciate this surplus step more than van Gogh. In truth, the concise description of the creative process he offered his brother was only intended to serve as a metaphor for something else. At the time he was trying desperately to discover his path in life ("What am I good for?" one letter pleaded) and though he couldn't quite see his way, he was convinced that it would become clear to him. It would become clear to him, he suggested to Theo, *just as* slowly but surely his rough draft turned into a sketch, and the sketch became a painting. The creative process he understood; there was a natural rhythm to it, like the rain. His hope was that his path would unfold by the very same method.

The path he had already set out on and recently abandoned had taken many twists and turns, and his service to God—which he was convinced was to be rendered through teaching and preaching—had proved a dismal failure. He had been dismissed from his parish post and refused admittance to theological school.

Now he was at a point of crisis. The fact that he used a painting analogy to illustrate the most difficult crossroad of his life might have provided him an important clue. But while still befuddled, he was de-

1. Vincent van Gogh to Theo van Gogh, July 1880, number 133. Letters may be freely used, in accordance with the Creative Commons license.

spondent; his soul kindled a great fire, he told Theo, but no one wanted to warm himself by it. Others looked at him on the outside and seeing only a bit of smoke coming from his chimney, dismissed him—and, consequently, missed the great fire.[2]

Despite his inner torment, there was a hint of the insight to come. "To try to understand," Vincent wrote to Theo, "the real significance of what the great artists, the serious masters, tell us in their masterpieces, *that* leads to God; one man wrote or told it in a book; another, in a picture."[3] After much prayer and pleading (and solace sought in a painting of Christ as a comforter to the brokenhearted), Vincent at last saw his path straighten before him: he was to serve God not as a preacher but as an artist. He believed that the sublime beauty in art, whether or not its artist was aware of it, came from God, and the work could then be used to unite God to man in a way his teaching and preaching never could. Uniting God and man was the intention of another artist, as I recall; in fact, the very *first* artist. Perhaps if she and Vincent share the same purpose, they will share the same joy at its consummation.

That is why the spiritual counterpart of the creative process does not end when the painting is hung or the poem recited. If our paths themselves are creative acts of God, then our *response* to finding that path and fulfilling that path is something more than the scientific model can contain. Its expression is what comprises the final layer of God's creative process. And what is the response?

To find out I look back at the words of David that allowed me to see our paths as creative acts in the first place: "The steps of a man are established by the LORD" (Ps 37:23a, NASB). Reviewing it again I realize I have captured only the first half of David's insight; there is a part b. After affirming that our steps are established (in the literal sense of being "created") by God, he adds: "And he delights in his way." In some versions it is God who is delighting and in others it is man. "His path blazed by God, he's happy," translates *The Message*. But what's most important is the response itself. It is the same spontaneous burst of emotion Wisdom displays at the creation of the world, the response that elicits her very first cartwheel: it is *delight*.

It is what caused the guests at Babette's feast to frolic like little lambs in the snow—even as it dissolved their long-held grudges. It is what

2. Ibid.

3. Van Gogh, *Complete Letters*, Letter 133.

made Alexander Graham Bell rise to his feet when Watson, in an adjoining room, clearly heard his words spoken into the telephone for the first time—drawing Aleck closer to his goal of helping those like his wife and mother who could not hear. Always the delight comes from a deep sense of connection, man with God, man with man. As it was in the creation of the world, delight is the consummation of the creative process, the reflex response to having participated in both path and passion.

In the Hebrew language the word *delight* doesn't just translate into pleasure or joy; it connotes a strong positive attraction for something. It differs from other words for this emotion by emphasizing *subjective* involvement, the expression of a deep feeling welling up from *within*. It even has a kinesthetic dimension that can be expressed through "bending" and "bowing." No wonder the old guests gamboled, Aleck sprung to his feet, and Wisdom turned a cartwheel.

But what about Van Gogh? What was his response? Stories of his emotional and mental struggles far outweigh the stories told of his devotion to God. And yet it was there, as he continued along his newfound path. Knowing the right road home and sometimes staggering drunkenly along it, as Tolstoy said of his own life, does not make the road a wrong one.

Three years after he discovered his road was to paint, Vincent wrote a letter to Theo about a day trip to Zweeloo, a village in the Netherlands. His letter sketches the scene around him—a little apple orchard; fields of young corn, the greenest of greens (did he experience Picasso's indigestion?); the sky a lilac-white he does not think can be captured in paint.[4] His sketches move from nature to people (he being "a little speck watching other little specks"): a ploughman hard at work, a little old woman at her spinning wheel, the return of the shepherd and his flock at dusk. Thus immersed in the scene around him he remembers neither to eat nor drink the entire day.

Taking in the rapid-fire exuberance of his brother's letter, Theo may have thought, "But what do you have to show for it?"

Vincent anticipates his question and answers it. He has brought home a ravenous hunger and a handful of rough sketches. But he has one thing more to show for his day, he assures his brother. For at last someone had come to warm herself by the great fire in his soul, and as the first artist, the gift she left was hers to give: delight.

4. Vincent van Gogh to Theo van Gogh, November 1883, number 340. Letters may be freely used, in accordance with the Creative Commons license.

PART FOUR

Finding the Place

12

Locale for Now: Carving Out Holy Spaces

Now my soul hath elbow-room.

William Shakespeare

I T IS A CONFESSION my husband does not expect to hear, divulged one evening before bed. "I am tired of having to talk myself down off the ledge every single day as I work," I say wearily. Even after adjusting for hyperbole, something he does expect to hear, he can tell I am serious, and he is concerned. Something is out of sync.

Every stage of the creative process has its own emotional barrier to overcome, but I have been through the worst of it, cleared nearly all of them. I am at a good place, with only a few chapters left to write in this book I've devoted nearly two years to. It is what we used to call "gravy" when I sold books door to door in college; those productive hours at the end of the day when Mr. and Mrs. Jones are both at home and objections are easily overcome and sales easily sopped up. From a spiritual stand-point, I am as close to delight as I will ever be. But instead, I am filled with anxiety and most of my emotional energy goes to self-talking my way out of panic in order to continue writing. I am in the solid stage of the creative process, but my will has turned to soup.

I have said that Wisdom's dream had given me a pattern, a place, and an alphabet of three. But despite my growing understanding of the divine pattern of creativity and my embrace of the roles of wisdom, understanding, and knowledge in the creative process, I have neglected the importance of *place*. Wisdom's first recorded interaction with the humankind she delights in is when she infuses Bezalel with the creativity ability to build a Holy Space, a place where God and humanity can draw closer together. In the same way, she carves out a holy space for each of us as we use our creative gifts to the same end. For each person a house is built, for each house rooms are filled with rare and beautiful treasures (Prov 24:3–4). Part of what is contained in these holy spaces, where Wisdom keeps her treasures stored, are the natural rhythms of a creative life. It was those rhythms I had failed to observe. Creativity has a cadence, and my own misstep had put me on the ledge.

NATURAL RHYTHMS

The first rhythm I had neglected was sleep. Of course, I didn't deliberately deprive myself of sleep, but when my husband, son, and daughter got sick one after another, resulting in weeks of ill health and upset schedules, I built up a considerable sleep debt. Instead of offsetting the deficit by sleeping in or napping, I decided to tackle my work day with whatever limited resources I had left. Chapters don't get written in your sleep, I reasoned. (Although I was willing to concede, from experience, that book outlines do.)

It is common sense that well-rested minds are better problem solvers, but there was a greater link between my lack of sleep and creative fatigue than I was first aware. Recent studies have shown that a good night's sleep is not only essential for tackling the problems that await you in the new day but for resolving those problems you went to bed with.[1] That means that sleep doesn't just refresh our minds so that we can think more clearly while we are awake, but our brains continue to work on problems even *as* we sleep. The advice to "sleep on it" has always had proverbial success, but now it has brain science to back it up. Here's why: Memories are restructured before they are stored and during sleep that restructuring may actually make problems easier to solve. What is creativity but inspired rearrangement? In addition the researchers found that sleeping deeply results in heightened insight. That's because memories are not only recombined during the deepest phase of sleep but covert thoughts and concepts come out of hiding, multiplying components and enhancing the connections that lead to creative insight.

Before the advent of sleep research, Thomas Edison had a hunch about the importance of sleep to creativity, although he took advantage of a different phase of the cycle, the drowsy state just before sleep takes over. This in-between phase, when dreams and reality intermix, is similar to what children experience when fully awake, a discovery that links

1. McCall, "Sleep a Must for Creative Thinking," para. 2.

this brain-wave pattern to the vivid imaginations of childhood.[2] (With adolescence comes a reduction in these same brain waves.) To take advantage of this transitional state between wakefulness and sleep, and the vivid imagery attached to it, Edison would sit in a chair, his arms on the arm rests, with a ball bearing in each hand. On the floor he placed two pie plates, directly below his closed hands. When he began to doze off, his hands would relax and the ball bearings would slip, clanging onto the pie plates below. Waking with a start, he would write down any ideas that came to mind. The inventor of the electric light bulb, the phonograph, and motion pictures, among other things, may have also inadvertently invented the power nap.

The occurrence of mysterious activity during sleep reminds me of the whimsical fairy tale of the poor cobbler and his wife by the Brothers Grimm. Devastated by poverty, the cobbler has just enough leather for one final pair of shoes. He carefully cuts out the pieces one evening in preparation for the next morning's sober work, places them on his workbench, and because he has a good conscience, falls into a deep sleep. When he awakes, readied for a full morning of cobbling, he finds the shoes are already neatly sewn together, with a mastery to match his own. The shoes fetch a higher price than usual, allowing the cobbler to buy leather for two more pairs of shoes. He again cuts out the pieces in the evening and goes to sleep. When he awakes, with the renewed vigor good fortune brings, he finds two pairs of shoes, expertly crafted. The pairs are quickly sold, and he is able to buy leather for four more pairs of shoes. On and on it goes, until the cobbler is a rich man. He and wife decide to sit up one night to see who it is who lends them a helping hand. At midnight two little men appear on the workbench and begin to work diligently, as they had each night while the cobbler slept, stitching, hammering, and arranging the various pieces until they fit together perfectly.

I would have fared much better had I taken this fabled course. If I had gone to bed with all my pieces carefully prepared, entrusting my work to the next morning and allowing myself to fall into a deep restorative sleep, I would have awakened to find that while I slept, the work was being done, the components combined and recombined, the insights risen to the surface and waiting for me on the workbench. Instead I had been working with no helpers, cobbling together a few uninspired words with the last scraps I had.

2. Goleman et al., *Creative Spirit*, 59.

The fairy tale ends when the cobbler and his wife make clothes for the little men, raising their esteem and liberating them from the workshop. But for us the elves never leave, never cease their work, as long as we respect the natural rhythm of sleep.

During this time I was out of step with another rhythm in my life, although its link to creativity is rarely noted. I had abandoned the ritual of my daily chores. Of course, there is no time and energy to mow the lawn or vacuum stairs when a child needs an X-ray or a husband is waiting for a prescription to be picked up. But regardless of circumstance, some experts advise creative people to *always* delegate these types of tasks to others, as a way to conserve mental energy, the way Einstein did by wearing the same clothes every day.

My experience proved otherwise. Order is naturally an important factor in clear thinking so if you are not going to maintain your living or working space, someone else probably should. But to farm out "menial" tasks to others is a lost opportunity. There is something grounding about fixing a toilet or scrubbing floors. These activities create an attachment to your immediate environment, a way to cultivate the sacred in the ordinary by tending thoughtfully to your holy space.

But it wasn't just attachment and order I missed. I missed *performing* the tasks themselves. The chores provided a needful change of pace from the intense mental focus required for writing. They also combined two variables I had come to depend on for creative incubation: a moving body and a wandering mind.

In some ways abandoning my chores backfired as much as neglecting sleep did; tasks that require some focus but not too much thought allow for the subconscious to work, to rearrange jumbled thoughts and memories the way sleep does. If you add movement the process is even more fruitful because physical motion facilitates creativity. Just this week a new study was published with findings to uphold my experience: a wandering mind is much more active than scientists realized, in fact, *more* active than when reasoning a complex problem. It appears that certain areas of the brain only work in unison during these times of unfocused thought.[3] But before daydreamers everywhere revel in their reveries, there is a caveat. Like the cobbler who carefully prepared his

3. Hotz, "A Wandering Mind," para. 8.

pieces of leather before going to bed, insight favors those with a prepared mind. Open-minded preparation first, then mental meandering.
But preparation without the mental reprieve had put me out of sync.
Once I resumed my daily chores, ideas begin to flow again. The mental
sluggishness, and sense of despair that accompanied it, disappeared.
Sweeping (with a simple stick and bristle broom) has become my favorite means of incubating insights, but any activity that combines movement with routine, whether it be gardening or cleaning or mowing the
lawn, reaps the same benefits.

Along the way I may have stumbled upon a method to harness my
mind-wandering much like Edison was able to harness his power-nap-
ping. This discovery was made when I taught an early-morning class at
the university and attempted to get ready without waking the rest of the
household. After showering, I'd lug my hairdryer, makeup, and clothes
downstairs, set a full-length mirror (also lugged) against the fireplace,
and sit on the floor in front of it so that I would have room to glance
down at my lecture notes beside me on the floor as I got ready. What I
noticed is the activity of getting ready, which required some focus but
little complex thought, gave me a heightened sense of awareness when
reviewing my notes. I was able to remember the material better than if
I had set aside time to read over my notes without the "distraction" of
getting ready. Once I started writing books, I continued to perform my
magician's trick, even setting up the same mirror in my bedroom to allow me to get ready by sitting on the floor. But instead of lecture notes I
now place beside me the writing I did the day before, carefully editing it
as I dry my hair and get ready for the day. This routine has become such
a natural and necessary rhythm that I never questioned why it worked
so well. Now, with this new research, I suspect that the task of getting
ready—like shaving or showering and other routine tasks—activates the
default network associated with daydreaming, and because I'm going
back and forth between a focused task and an unfocused one, I'm able to
take advantage of the more active state of a wandering mind. It's as if I'm
able to see my work in 3-D, from a global perspective that veers from the
straight line I usually follow when I edit. Sometimes when I get stuck I
go back upstairs to my magic mirror and go through the motions of my
morning prep (including the editing) to get unstuck. I wonder, though,
if the larger lesson here is that creativity resists the needless partitioning

of life (into work, play, routine) and flourishes best when woven into the fabric of my day, a careful blending of the meaningful and the ordinary.

One of Einstein's biographers lamented the fact that the physicist's attention was diverted from serious work by household tasks that went beyond which sweater and pair of pants to wear. He cites as an example Einstein's routine of rocking his baby in the carriage while he worked at the kitchen table of his small apartment. With one hand he wrote what would become his classic papers and with the other hand he rocked the cradle, back and forth, back and forth. What would Einstein have accomplished if he could focus on his work without the distraction, the biographer pondered? My answer is, "Perhaps less." I think the rhythm helped him; not just the back-and-forth sway of the baby carriage, and the lulling of the child inside it, but the desire to observe and honor the natural rhythms of his life.

NATURE'S RHYTHMS

During this time of prolonged sickness in my family, I also missed out on my daily walks around the neighborhood, and while the lack of exercise was no boon to my health, the real cost to me was something else. The truth is if I had done the walking on the treadmill at the gym the result would have been the same. What I needed was an audience with the one Emily Dickinson dubbed "the gentlest mother." I needed time outdoors, with nature.

The restorative effect of "the gentlest mother" has been celebrated for centuries in poetry and literature, but now scientists have taken pains to quantify it. Stephen Kaplan is one of them, a psychologist and engineer at the University of Michigan who has developed a theory that immersion in nature has a restorative effect on attention and, as a result, on all kinds of other cognitive abilities, including creativity. (His concept is called attention restoration theory, aptly simplified into ART.) The findings of related studies are both fascinating and disturbing: hospital patients recover more quickly when they can see trees from their windows, children with attention deficit disorder have fewer symptoms and are better able to focus in natural settings, and one study found there was less domestic violence in apartments in a housing project that had views of greenery.

Even the study I referred to in chapter 7 about the brain benefits of walking vs. jogging had an addendum: the benefits depend on *where* you walk. Study participants who walked through the busy downtown area of a city came back to the cognitive tasks for memory and attention mentally depleted and in bad moods; in contrast, those who took a walk in the park were refreshed, in good moods, and showed a marked improvement on tests for memory and attention. The study's authors believe the difference can be explained by the attention centers of the brain: a city setting bombards the brain with complex and confusing patterns that require directed attention; a walk in the park, still with plenty to attend to but none of it overwhelming, requires less mental effort and has a restorative effect on the brain.[4] Such "locomotion in nature" (translated as walking, biking, etc.) was also found to be a powerful means of avoiding burnout, as opposed to watching television, which was the quickest route to it. Studies with children, whose imaginations are less taxed and attention less strained than their grown-up counterparts, show an even greater link between exposure to nature and a boost in creativity. And while we know that insight favors a prepared mind, it also appears to bless a contented one: people in good moods are more likely to experience insight.

That doesn't mean we should all pack up and move to Walden Pond. Even a few minutes in a natural setting has a dramatic effect, as do glimpses of nature from a window. A study by Kaplan's wife Rachel found a triad of benefits for office workers who had a view of nature: they enjoyed their jobs more, they experienced better health, and they reported greater life satisfaction.[5] The governing body in Denmark is ahead of the curve; the Scandinavian country has in place a law that every school child and working adult be able to see nature from their seat or workspace.[6] (That may explain Denmark's current ranking as "the happiest place in the world.")

The best solution is sometimes the simplest one. Forgo the energy drinks, the memory-enhancing supplements, the brain-boosting online quizzes. Take a walk in the park instead. Look out the window. You can also bring some of nature indoors. One study showed that kids surrounded by natural wood and sunlight were more creative when doing projects than were kids surrounded by drywall and plastic. In "The Garden," seventeenth-century poet Andrew Marvel writes of the quiet

4. Bowman, "Walking Has Brain Benefits," para. 11.

5. Clay, "Green is Good for You," 40.

6. Hannaford, *Smart Moves*, 150.

and innocence of nature fostering "a green thought in a green shade," and modern author Thomas Moore wisely applies that sentiment to our times. If we insist on surrounding ourselves with plastic ferns, he says, we do so to similar effect: we will think only plastic thoughts.[7]

Scientists concede that the link between nature and mental restoration is already intuitive to most people. Indeed, it shouldn't surprise us that the craftsmanship that made the morning stars rejoice and Wisdom twirl in delight would be an essential rhythm in our lives, especially in bolstering creative ability. But the restoration doesn't just reach the mind; it seeps into the soul as well. When the psalmist David wrote of soul-recovery in the twenty-third Psalm, he did so in the context of nature: "He makes me lie down in green pastures, he leads me beside quiet waters, he restores my soul." Nature heals the mind and the soul.

I opened this chapter with the last words of King John of England, at least those put in his mouth by Shakespeare. In the last scene of the play King John is dying and requests to be taken outside. He is carried in a chair to the abbey's orchard where, surrounded by its lush trees, he declares, "Now my soul hath elbow-room." It could not be coaxed to come out any other way, he says.

In cultivating our own holy spaces, then, it's important to remember that they are meant to be fashioned into the woodwork of a much larger holy space, the woodwork that is the handiwork of God.

Once I understood that, and my own natural rhythms were restored, I was able to step down off the ledge and find my way back into the shelter of my holy space, with elbowroom.

7. Moore, *Care of the Soul*, 180.

13

Locale for Later: Cultivating the Thin Places

*We . . . will arrive where we started
And know the place for the first time.*

T. S. Eliot

THE ELBOW ROOM NEEDED in a holy space isn't of a physical nature only; daily rhythms, restorative sleep, and exposure to nature aren't the only ways to "make room." There is a spiritual component to the idea of *place*; there must be something there that makes the place *holy*. In writing about wisdom, Howard Gardner pointed out its unique properties in relation to his other areas of study. Wisdom is distinct, he wrote, because "neither intelligence nor creativity . . . reserves a place for silence, for quiet, for resignation."[1]

He·didn't see wisdom's bent toward silence and quiet and resignation as a natural part of the creative process, and yet it is inherent in the spiritual counterpart, in the divine pattern of creativity. It is the most important aspect of a holy space, the most carefully crafted of Wisdom's treasures.

Every day science provides a truer picture of real productivity, and the findings are shattering the assumptions of a culture ever on the go. It was once a badge of honor to exist on little sleep; it was once the scourge of the schoolroom to be caught daydreaming. It was once a sign of weakness to take a nap or to walk in the park instead of working through lunch. But it has always been built into the framework of holy spaces to stop, to rest, to reflect. If the purpose of a holy space is to draw God and humanity closer together, that connection cannot be forged through

1. Gardner, *Intelligence Reframed*, 134.

noise and confusion. "Nothing in all creation is so like God as stillness," wrote Meister Eckhart, so that drawing close to God means being still.[2]

Being still is not the needful inertia I wrote about earlier or the relaxed receptivity of incubation; it is an active posture of mindful reflection, contemplation, and prayer.

LIFE IMITATES ART

Part of what makes a space holy is cultivating *thin places*. A thin place, from the Celtic tradition, is a locale or junction where the veil between heaven and earth is at its thinnest; for the ancient Celts this included not only natural landscapes that inspired awe but holy places made by human hands. Like the state just before sleep when dreams and reality mix, a thin place is where the sacred and the ordinary become for a moment indistinguishable.

Reading is one of the ways I cultivate thin places, and if I can read in a natural setting, so much the better. During a week at the beach, I began reading two books to attenuate the veil, one fiction and the other nonfiction. Serendipitously (serendipity is rife in thin places), there was a question posed in the nonfiction book that the make-believe book was able to answer for me. The first book was N. T. Wright's *Surprised by Hope*, a work that challenges the reader to forgo thoughts of an afterlife of cloud-sitting, harp-playing, and wings-earning. Instead he opens up the true biblical picture of afterlife in terms of God's promise of a new heaven and a new earth—where more elements of this life will continue than we were led to believe in Sunday school. The main lesson for me: There is continuity between what we do now and what we will do for all eternity.

Wright explains: "What you *do* in the present," and here his list sounds like the various ways Wisdom expresses herself, "—by painting, preaching, singing, sewing, praying, teaching, building hospitals, digging wells, campaigning for justice, writing poems, caring for the needy, loving your neighbor as yourself—*will last into God's future*. These activities are not simply ways of making the present life a little less beastly, a little more bearable, until the day when we leave it behind altogether."[3]

---

2. Eckhart, *Meister Eckhart*, 243.

3. This quote and the two that follow are from Wright, *Surprised by Hope*, 193, 209, and 161, respectively.

I was especially taken with his idea of how creative works crafted here might transfer to the hereafter: "I don't know what musical instruments we shall have to play Bach in God's new world, though I'm sure Bach's music will be there . . . I do not know how the painting an artist paints today in prayer and wisdom will find a place in God's new world," but find a place it will.

It was that rumination about an artist and his painting that was addressed by the second book, a collection of fairy tales and short stories by J. R. R. Tolkien. The most illuminating story in the collection, "Leaf by Niggle," was an anomaly for Tolkien, who like Beethoven, was a master of revision, a compulsive rewriter. But this short story about a painter was the boon of a good night's sleep; Tolkien awoke one morning with the story complete in his head, as if it had been carefully stitched together by elves as he slept. During that time he was struggling with the enormity of the task of writing *The Lord of the Rings*, which he had just begun, paralyzed by the idea that the series would never be completed. (It's possible then that the story had been the work of hobbits, not elves.)

Niggle is a simple man, living in a small house in the countryside, a painter whose work is continually hindered by a "crop of interruptions." The crop includes jury duty, house repairs, visitors, and especially requests from his neighbor Parish, who is lame. Niggle's principle creative work begins when he paints a leaf caught in the wind, but it soon grows into a tree; the tree grows so large Niggle builds a tall shed to house it and needs a ladder to reach the canvas. Niggle is also aware he will be called on to make a long journey soon and dreads the idea, especially as there are aspects of his massive tree painting he will only have time to "hint at." Parish's wife becomes ill, and he asks Niggle to go for the doctor and leave a note with the builder, since Parish's roof also needs repair. En route on his bicycle to fulfill the requests, Niggle sees clearly in his mind's eye how to represent an element in his painting (no doubt inspired by his "locomotion in nature"), but worries he will not have a chance to try it out and blames Parish for the inconvenience. Soaked to the skin by the same storm that knocked the tiles off Parish's roof, Niggle becomes ill and is at last called on to make his long journey.

At the end of the story Niggle arrives by train at his destination and finds a bicycle just like the one he left behind; a label is affixed with his name on it. He begins to ride the bicycle over a majestic sweep of grass (as if in a dream he can see each blade distinctly) until he is overcome by a "great green shadow." He looks up to see what has cast the shadow and then falls off his bicycle.

Before him stands "the Tree, his Tree, finished. If you could say that of a Tree that was alive, its leaves opening, its branches growing and bending in the wind that Niggle had so often felt or guessed, and had so often failed to catch."[4]

Niggle lifts his arms to the heavens and shouts, "It's a gift!" Yes, it is a gift, both the creative ability and the enlivened result. There is a connection between this holy space and the holy space in which he painted his tree; he has arrived where he started and knows the place for the first time.

All the leaves he has ever painted are there and even those that he might have painted if he had had time. He has a heightened understanding that the most beautiful of the leaves have somehow been produced in collaboration with Parish, even though the soliciting neighbor had never lifted a paintbrush. Only then does Niggle realize the importance of what he dismissed as "interruptions." They were essentials, part of the natural rhythms of his life. They were as important to his work as the paint and canvas, as rocking a baby is to breakthroughs in physics.

Niggle also learns that honoring his life's natural rhythms would not have kept him from completing his work; there was time enough (if it could be called that) now. He would continue to nourish his tree in a way he never could before.

Is it possible, Tolkien is asking, that there is a creative link between the here and the hereafter? Does a painting an artist paints today in prayer and wisdom find a place in God's new world? Perhaps life not only imitates art, as Oscar Wilde observed, but the afterlife imitates it as well. Imagine the possibility that our creative gifts will be, in N. T. Wright's words, "enhanced and ennobled and given back to us" for all eternity. It makes our responsibility to discover and hone these gifts even greater. It makes the privilege of using them even more profound.

THE DREAM

In a letter to an acquaintance, Tolkien explained that he wrote the story about Niggle to try to show through allegory how creative acts "might come to be taken up into Creation in some plane."[5] Indeed, Niggle's tree

---

4. Tolkien, "Leaf by Niggle," 302–3.
5. Tolkien, *Letters*, 321.

is fully realized, fully alive—the tree he painted in the holy space of his tall shed now provides a respite for others en route to the Mountains (Tolkien's version of the holy space of eternity), including Parish, who dies shortly after Niggle does. It was Tolkien's belief that only God truly creates and for those of us who attempt to "rearrange the something of God," as I put it earlier, there are only two recourses: you can echo God's creation or make a mockery of it.

That is what I've discovered, too, during the past two years as the meaning of my dream, itself the boon of a good night's sleep, has carefully unfolded. I have discovered the ways in which God echoes. Not only how God echoes the first act of creation, but also his first dwelling place on earth. Wisdom continues to carve out holy spaces to store her gifts.

It is these holy spaces that determine whether the creative act is an echo or a mockery. It is the thin places—forged through rest, reflection, prayer—that rearrange the something of God into something that honors him, in this world and quite possibly the next, where there is no longer a veil that separates.

The story of Niggle had been given to Tolkien as he slept both to assure him (there is time enough to create) and to admonish him (honor the daily rhythms of your life). My dream had been given to me for the same reasons, but at the time I only saw the admonition: open the room, clear the dust, feed the animals. I am back where I started, but now, like Niggle, I see what is casting the shadow. It is Wisdom's house; both the materials and the plan to build a creative life had been there all along, hidden in a single passage of Scripture. The assurance is that there is a comprehensive blueprint, a fully developed method of cultivating the creative spirit in everyday life, practically and spiritually. The room, the fine furniture, the ladle on the mantle, the intricate interworking of wisdom, knowledge and understanding; they're all here.

But I know the place for the first time.

14

Resources

Everybody is a genius. But if you judge a fish by its ability to climb a tree, it will live its whole life believing that it is stupid.

Albert Einstein

I PROVIDE THE FOLLOWING inventory with the disclaimer that Howard Gardner was not in favor of paper-and-pencil assessments of his groundbreaking theory of multiple intelligences. Since his research was, in part, a reaction against such measures, Gardner opts for other ways to evaluate: toss the pencil and set a child loose in a museum. It may be too late for most of us to be set loose in a children's museum, but Gardner also suggests relying on the testimony of friends as well as observing the person in the context of a particular intelligence (allow a person to find his way around an unfamiliar terrain to gauge spatial intelligence, for example).

Still, this inventory is a helpful starting point.[1]

---

1. The Rogers Indicator of Multiple Intelligences (RIMI) is a tool created by J. Keith Rogers, PhD, formerly a professor at Brigham Young University, P.O. Box 127, Albion, ID 83311. Used with permission.

For an online version of the Rogers Indicator of Multiple Intelligences (RIMI) with automatic scoring: http://www.personal.psu.edu/bxb11/MI/MIQuiz.htm.

The Rogers Indicator of Multiple Intelligences

QUESTIONS	Rarely 1	Occasionally 2	Sometimes 3	Usually 4	Almost Always 5
1. I am careful about the direct and implied meanings of the words I use in speaking and writing.	O	O	O	O	O
2. I appreciate a wide variety of music.	O	O	O	O	O
3. People come to me when they need help with math problems or any calculations.	O	O	O	O	O
4. In my mind, I can visualize clear, precise, sharp images.	O	O	O	O	O
5. I am physically well coordinated.	O	O	O	O	O
6. I understand why I believe and behave the way I do.	O	O	O	O	O
7. I understand the moods, temperaments, values, and intentions of others, even when they are hidden.	O	O	O	O	O
8. I am intrigued by systems of classifying dinosaurs, plants, birds, fishes, etc. or things such as highways, storms, etc.	O	O	O	O	O
9. I confidently express myself well in words, written or spoken, privately or publicly.	O	O	O	O	O
10. I understand the basic precepts of music such as rhythm, harmony, chords, and keys.	O	O	O	O	O

QUESTIONS	Rarely 1	Occasionally 2	Sometimes 3	Usually 4	Almost Always 5
11. When I have a problem, I use a logical, analytical, step-by-step process to arrive at a solution.	O	O	O	O	O
12. I have a good sense of direction for north, south, etc.	O	O	O	O	O
13. I have skill in handling objects such as scissors, hammers, scalpels, paintbrushes, knitting needles, pliers, wrenches, toys, game pieces, etc.	O	O	O	O	O
14. My self-understanding helps me to make wise decisions for my life.	O	O	O	O	O
15. I am able to influence other individuals to believe and/or behave in response to my own beliefs, preferences, and desires.	O	O	O	O	O
16. I am a "born naturalist" and have always had high interest in and interaction with the natural world whenever and wherever I could.	O	O	O	O	O
17. I am grammatically accurate and sensitive.	O	O	O	O	O
18. I like to compose or create music or rhythms.	O	O	O	O	O
19. I am rigorous and skeptical in accepting facts, arguments, reasons, and principles.	O	O	O	O	O

QUESTIONS	Rarely 1	Occasionally 2	Sometimes 3	Usually 4	Almost Always 5
20. I am good at putting together jigsaw puzzles, and understanding instructions, patterns, or blueprints.	O	O	O	O	O
21. I excel in physical activities such as sports, dance, orienteering, riding horses, games, climbing, etc.	O	O	O	O	O
22. My ability to understand my own emotions helps me to decide whether or how to be involved in various situations.	O	O	O	O	O
23. I would like to be involved in "helping" professions such as teaching, therapy, or counseling, or to do work such as political or religious leadership.	O	O	O	O	O
24. I am very interested in things such as farming, gardening, hunting, fishing, bird-watching, forestry, and ranching.	O	O	O	O	O
25. I am able to use spoken or written words to influence or persuade others effectively.	O	O	O	O	O
26. I enjoy performing music, such as singing or playing a musical instrument for an audience.	O	O	O	O	O
27. I require scientific explanations of physical realities.	O	O	O	O	O
28. I can use graphs and maps easily and accurately.	O	O	O	O	O

QUESTIONS	Rarely 1	Occasionally 2	Sometimes 3	Usually 4	Almost Always 5
29. I work well with my hands, as would an electrician, seamstress, plumber, tailor, mechanic, carpenter, assembler, etc.	O	O	O	O	O
30. I am aware of the complexity of my own feelings, emotions, and beliefs in various circumstances.	O	O	O	O	O
31. I am able to work as an effective intermediary in helping other individuals and groups to solve their problems.	O	O	O	O	O
32. I respect studies such as oceanography, botany, entomology, herpetology, ornithology, and zoology.	O	O	O	O	O
33. I am sensitive to the sounds, rhythms, inflections, and meters of words, especially as found in poetry.	O	O	O	O	O
34. I have a strong sense of musical rhythm.	O	O	O	O	O
35. I would like to do the work of people such as chemists, engineers, physicists, astronomers, or mathematicians.	O	O	O	O	O
36. I am able to produce graphic depictions of the spatial world as in drawing, painting, sculpting, drafting, or mapmaking.	O	O	O	O	O

QUESTIONS	Rarely 1	Occasionally 2	Sometimes 3	Usually 4	Almost Always 5
37. I relieve stress or find fulfillment in physical activities such as hiking, canoeing, walking, sports, or cycling.	O	O	O	O	O
38. My inner self is my ultimate source of strength, renewal, and motivation.	O	O	O	O	O
39. I understand what motivates others even when they are trying to hide their motivations.	O	O	O	O	O
40. As a child, I was fascinated with the insects, plants, birds, trees, snakes, frogs, flowers, leaves, lizards, bugs, snails, etc., in my natural environment.	O	O	O	O	O
41. I enjoy reading frequently and widely.	O	O	O	O	O
42. I have a strong sense of musical pitch.	O	O	O	O	O
43. I find personal satisfaction in dealing with numbers.	O	O	O	O	O
44. In my mind, I can see patterns and relationships. I can remember, imagine, and invent what things look like or might look like in reality.	O	O	O	O	O
45. I have quick and accurate physical reflexes and responses in recreation, games, dancing, etc.	O	O	O	O	O
46. I am confident in my own opinions and beliefs and am not easily swayed by others.	O	O	O	O	O

QUESTIONS	Rarely 1	Occasionally 2	Sometimes 3	Usually 4	Almost Always 5
47. I am comfortable and confident with groups of people in most circumstances.	O	O	O	O	O
48. I have a "green thumb" and am often a resource to others who care about the natural environment.	O	O	O	O	O
49. My "body language" is a vital method of communication.	O	O	O	O	O
50. I am affected both emotionally and intellectually by music of various kinds at different times.	O	O	O	O	O
51. I prefer questions that have definite "right" and "wrong" answers.	O	O	O	O	O
52. I can accurately estimate distances and other measurements.	O	O	O	O	O
53. I have accurate aim when throwing balls or in archery, shooting, golf, volleyball, tennis, etc.	O	O	O	O	O
54. My feelings, beliefs, attitudes, opinions, and emotions are my own responsibility.	O	O	O	O	O
55. I have a large circle of close associates.	O	O	O	O	O
56. I have or would like to have expertise in the recognition and classification of flora and fauna (plants and animals) and other things in my natural environment.	O	O	O	O	O

INDICATOR SCORES

DIRECTIONS: In the chart below, the numbers are the same as the statement numbers in the survey. You made a rating judgment for each statement. Now, place the numbers that correspond to your ratings (1–5, Rarely to Almost Always) in the spaces below. Then add down the columns and write the totals at the bottom to determine your score in each of the seven categories.

Linguistic	Musical	Logical-Math	Spatial	Bodily-Kinesthetic	Intrapersonal	Interpersonal	Naturalist
1 ___	2 ___	3 ___	4 ___	5 ___	6 ___	7 ___	8 ___
9 ___	10 ___	11 ___	12 ___	13 ___	14 ___	15 ___	16 ___
17 ___	18 ___	19 ___	20 ___	21 ___	22 ___	23 ___	24 ___
25 ___	26 ___	27 ___	28 ___	29 ___	30 ___	31 ___	32 ___
33 ___	34 ___	35 ___	36 ___	37 ___	38 ___	39 ___	40 ___
41 ___	42 ___	43 ___	44 ___	45 ___	46 ___	47 ___	48 ___
49 ___	50 ___	51 ___	52 ___	53 ___	54 ___	55 ___	56 ___

TOTALS:

___   ___   ___   ___   ___   ___   ___   ___

INTERPRETATION OF SCORES

To some degree we possess all of these intelligences, or areas of creativity, and all can be enhanced. We are each a unique blend of all eight; however, we all differ in the degree to which we prefer and have the competence to use each of the intelligences. Below are presented interpretations for the scores in the three ranges of low, moderate, and high.

Score Intensity of Preference and/or Competence

7–15: Low Intensity

You tend to "avoid" it and are probably uncomfortable when required to use it. This is considered a tertiary preference (3). This intelligence probably is not one of your favorites. In most circumstances, you lack confidence and will go out of your way to avoid situations involving intensive exercise of this intelligence. Your competence is probably relatively low. Unless you are unusually motivated, gaining expertise might be frustrating and likely would require great effort. All intelligences, including this one, can be enhanced throughout your lifetime.

16–26: Moderate Intensity

You tend to "accept" it or use it with some comfort and ease. This is considered a secondary preference (2). You could take or leave the application or use of this intelligence. Though you accept it, you do not necessarily prefer to employ it. But, on the other hand, you would not necessarily avoid using it. This may be because you have not developed your ability, or because you have a moderate preference for this intelligence. Your competence is probably moderate also. Gaining expertise would be satisfying but would require considerable effort.

27–35: High Intensity

You tend to "prefer" it and use it often with comfort and facility. This is considered a primary preference (1). You enjoy using this intelligence. Applying it is fun. You are excited and challenged by it, perhaps even fascinated. You prefer this intelligence. Given the opportunity, you will usually select it. Everyone knows you love it. Your competence is probably relatively high if you have had opportunities to develop it. Becoming an expert should be rewarding and fulfilling and will probably require little effort compared to a moderate or low preference.

REVIEW OF MULTIPLE INTELLIGENCES

Musical: This intelligence involves skill in the performance, composition, and appreciation of musical patterns and can be seen in musicians and composers.

Bodily-kinesthetic: Involves using one's whole body or part of the body (e.g., hand or mouth) to solve problems or fashion products. Obvious examples include dancers, actors, and athletes; less obvious, craftsmen, surgeons, and mechanics.

Spatial: Involves the ability to recognize and manipulate the patterns of wide spaces as well as the patterns of more confined areas. Those who operate wide spaces include navigators and pilots; those who manipulate more confined spaces include sculptors, chess players, and architects.

Gardner called these next two intelligences the personal intelligences. Although each of the intelligences has an emotional component, these two are the most firmly rooted in emotional perception.

Interpersonal: Involves the capacity to understand the intentions, motivations, and desires of other people, resulting in the ability to work effectively with others, as do salespeople, teachers, religious leaders, and politicians.

Intrapersonal: Involves the ability to understand oneself, one's own desires, fears, and capacities and using that understanding to effectively regulate one's life. This intelligence is evident in philosophers, psychologists, and theologians.

And, of course, Gardner includes these two, the only two *traditionally* linked to intelligence:

Linguistic: Involves sensitivity to spoken and written language, the ability to learn languages, the capacity to use language to accomplish certain goals. This intelligence can be seen in lawyers, speakers, and writers.

Logical-mathematical: Involves the capacity to analyze problems logically, carry out mathematical operations, and investigate issues scientifically. It also includes the ability to detect patterns, using logic and numbers to make connections and understand information. This intelligence can be seen in mathematicians, scientists, and economists, and also in researchers and detectives.

This intelligence was recently added to the list:

Naturalist: Involves an understanding of the living world and the ability to recognize and classify the components of the environment. It also includes the skill to care for or interact with living creatures. While most apparent in biologists and environmentalists, the naturalist intelligence can also be seen in farmers, gardeners, and cooks.

CAREER OR END-STATES OF THE INTELLIGENCES

Careers or End-States of the Musical Intelligence[2]

- audio-video technician
- band member
- choir or choral director
- choreographer
- conductor
- composer
- critic
- dancer
- disc or/and video jockey
- early childhood educator
- figure skater
- group singer
- instrument maker/repairer/salesperson/technician
- instrumental instructor/musician
- instrumentalist
- manager
- music copyist/critic/teacher/therapist
- musical arranger/performer
- musician
- piano tuner
- professional performer
- promoter

2. This and the following lists compiled by Clifford Morris, "Some General Occupations Needing Howard Gardner's Multiple Intelligences," http://www.igs.net/~cmorris/smo_comments.html.

- recording engineer/technician
- rock group
- singer
- solo singer
- song writer
- sound engineer
- teacher
- violinist

Careers or End-States of the Bodily-Kinesthetic Intelligence

- acrobat
- actor
- actress
- aerobics instructor
- architect
- artisans
- artistic painter
- assembler
- athlete
- ballet dancer
- building trade person
- carpenter
- choreographer
- clown
- coach
- commercial artist
- construction worker
- craftsperson
- dancer

- drama coach
- engineer
- equestrian
- ergonomist
- factory worker
- farmer
- firefighter
- forest ranger
- gymnast
- instrumental musician
- inventor
- jeweler
- jockey
- juggler
- magician
- manual laborer
- mason
- massage therapist
- mechanic
- mime
- model
- physical therapist
- physical education teacher
- physiotherapist
- pianist
- recreational worker
- rodeo rider
- sculptor
- stunt people

- swimming instructor
- surgeon
- trainer
- transport driver
- welder

Careers or End-States of the Spatial Intelligence

- advertiser
- architect
- artist
- art teacher/therapist
- builder
- carpenter
- cartographer
- chess player
- coach
- commercial artist
- computer-aided designer/computer programmer/computer specialist
- craftsperson
- decorator
- dentist
- drafting engineer/technician
- engineer
- fashion designer
- film director/editor
- fine artist
- furniture restorer
- geographer
- geometrician

- graphic artist/designer
- guide
- hairstylist
- hunter
- industrial design
- interior decorator/designer
- inventor
- landscape architect/designer
- machinist
- makeup artist
- mechanic
- mold designer
- navigator
- outdoor guide
- painter
- photographer
- pilot
- ranger
- sailor
- scout
- sculptor
- seamstress
- set designer
- sign painter
- surgeon
- surveyor
- tailor
- tour guide
- urban planner

- visual artist
- web developer

Careers or End-States of the Interpersonal Intelligence

- administrator
- anthropologist
- arbitrator
- bartender
- business person
- chess player
- childcare worker
- clergy person
- coach
- community organizer
- consumer service advocate
- counselor
- consultant
- daycare worker
- food server
- homemaker
- manager
- mediator
- nurse
- personnel worker
- police officer
- politician
- personnel officer
- probation officer
- psychologist

- psychotherapist
- public relations consultant/officer/person/promoter
- receptionist
- recreation assistant
- religious leader
- salesperson
- school principal
- secretary
- social director/leader/worker
- sociologist
- teacher
- teacher's aid/assistant
- therapist
- travel agent/counselor
- waiter
- waitress

Careers or End-States of the Intrapersonal Intelligence

- administrator
- actor
- anthropologist
- arbitrator
- artist
- businessperson
- clergy
- coach
- computer games developer
- consultant
- counselor

- creative writer
- daycare worker
- entrepreneur
- fitness instructor
- food server
- guru
- home support aide
- leadership trainer
- manager
- mediator
- minister
- novelist
- nurse
- personnel officer
- philosopher
- police officer
- politician
- program planner
- psychiatrist
- psychologist/psychology teacher
- psychotherapist
- public relations officer
- receptionist
- religious leader
- researcher
- sage
- salesperson
- self-employed person
- social director/worker

- sociologist
- spiritual counselor
- talent agent
- teacher assistant
- theologian
- theorist
- therapist
- vocational instructor
- wellness instructor
- writer

Careers or End-States of the Linguistic Intelligence

- archivist
- attorney
- author
- call center operator
- comedian
- copywriter
- curator
- editor
- English teacher
- historian
- interpreter
- journalist
- lawyer
- legal assistant
- librarian
- manager
- novelist

- online copy editor
- orator
- philosopher
- playwright
- poet
- politician
- proofreader
- psychotherapist
- public speaker
- public relations person
- radio/television announcer
- reporter
- sales person
- secretary
- social scientist
- speech pathologist/speech therapist assistant
- storyteller
- supervisor
- talk-show host
- teacher
- technical writer
- tour guide/travel counselor
- translator
- typist
- writer

Careers or End-States of the Logical-Mathematical Intelligence

- accountant
- actuary

- analyst
- astronomer
- auditor
- banker
- biologist
- bookkeeper
- chemist
- chess player
- city planner
- computer analyst/programmer/systems analyst
- cook
- database administrator/database programmer
- economist
- engineer
- financial service
- instrumentation technician
- inventor
- investment broker
- lawyer
- paralegal secretary
- logician
- mathematician
- mechanic
- mechanical engineer
- microbiologist
- payroll person (clerk or/and supervisor)
- pharmacist
- physician
- physicist

- programmer
- purchasing agent
- records clerk
- researcher
- science teacher
- scientist
- statistician
- stockbroker
- tax accountant
- technician
- technologist
- travel agent
- underwriter

Careers or End-States of the Naturalist Intelligence

- agricultural engineer/agricultural worker
- animal care technician/animal handler/animal trainer
- anthropologist
- aquaculture laborer
- astronomer
- beachcomber
- biologist
- botanist
- chef
- climatologist
- conservationist
- dog groomer/dog keeper
- ecologist
- entomologist

- environmental scientist
- ethologist (one who examines the scientific study of animal behavior, especially their habitats)
- farmer
- forester
- gardener
- geologist
- landscape architect/artist/gardener
- meteorologist
- navigator
- oceanographer
- ornithologist
- paleontologist
- park ranger
- rancher
- sailor
- scout
- veterinarian
- weather tracking specialist
- wildlife illustrator
- zoo keeper
- zoologist

ADDITIONAL MOVEMENTS TO ENHANCE CREATIVE THINKING (DISGUISED AS REGULAR EXERCISE)

While the set of movements outlined in chapter 7 are the ones I use on a daily basis, there are two additional Brain Gym techniques I would add to that list, because the science applies even if the movements are hidden in familiar exercises.

The Calf Pump

Runners typically stretch their calf muscles before or after a run to avoid injury. But a calf stretch has application to creative thinking as well. Stress can trigger a reflex that shortens calf muscles, readying the body for fight or flight. The tendon guard reflex is meant to provide short-term protection of tendons and muscles but when stress extends the protection, the reflex can put the body in a perpetual state of alert, keeping neck and back muscles in a locked position and decreasing the flow of cerebral spinal fluid. To relax the calf and associated muscles—and for thinking that flows freely—do the following exercise:

Standing

The standing calf pump can be done holding the back of a chair or with hands pressed against a wall, arms straight. Keeping the torso upright and with feet shoulder-width apart, extend one foot with the heel up about 12 inches from the other foot. Take a deep breath and as you exhale, lower the heel of the back foot to the ground while bending the front knee forward. Remember to keep your torso upright and resist leaning forward. Hold for 30 seconds and do the same stretch on the opposite leg.

Dr. Hannaford uses calf-stretching exercises quite a bit with her special needs students and has discovered a link between shortened calf muscles and speech impairment.[3] She surmises that special needs children are in a perpetual state of stress in academic settings, so that the survival response (the tendon guard reflex) is prolonged. She has linked these calf-lengthening exercises with improvement in learning and especially in speech development.

Sitting

You can also do this exercise less conspicuously (at a desk or cubicle, or if need be, in the middle of a tense meeting around a conference table) while sitting. If possible, extend your legs straight out in front of you, parallel to the floor. Point your toes toward you; hold the stretch for several seconds. Now point your toes away from you and hold. Do this several times to relax the calf muscles.

3. Hannaford, *Smart Moves*, 163. Brain Gym® movements used with permission from Paul and Gail Dennison.

On a Step

You can also do this stretch on a step, which is my preferred way of relaxing my calf muscles. Stand with both feet on the step, with the balls of the feet firmly on the step and the heels over the edge. You may want to hold on to a banister (if available) for support. Raise your heels so that you are on your tiptoes; hold for a moment. Then drop your heels below the step. You will feel a deep stretch. Repeat several times to lengthen the calf muscles.

The Sit-Up Meets the Cross Crawl

This next movement is both a variation of the Cross Crawl exercise and a fancified sit-up. Lie on your back with your hands behind your head. Lift your shoulders off the floor and draw your knees up to your chest. Twist to bring your right elbow to your left knee and then your left elbow to your right knee. Do this slowly and rhythmically just as you did the standing Cross Crawl.

This exercise carries the same benefits as other cross-lateral movements while relaxing the lower back and strengthening the core. The result: clearer thinking, tighter abs.

FURTHER READING

Further Reading about Brain Gym

Hannaford, Carla. *Smart Moves*. Arlington, VA: Great Ocean, 1995.

Dennison, Paul E., and Gail E. Dennison. *Brain Gym: Simple Activities for Whole Brain Learning*. Ventura, CA: Edu-Kinesthetics, Inc., 1986.

http://www.braingym.org/

Further Reading about Creativity

Goleman, Daniel, et al. *The Creative Spirit*. New York: Plume, 1993.

Csikszentmihalyi, Mihaly. *Creativity*. New York: HarperCollins, 1996.

Gardner, Howard. *Intelligence Reframed*. New York: Basic, 1999.

Michalko, Michael. *Cracking Creativity*. Berkeley, CA: Ten Speed, 2001.

Pink, Daniel H. *A Whole New Mind*. New York: Riverhead, 2005.

Acknowledgments

SOME TIME AFTER COMPLETING the manuscript for this book, I began to read for the first time A. W. Tozer's classic *The Pursuit of God*. There are many worthy insights in this book, but I was most struck by his depiction of what he called God's "speaking Voice." He draws a distinction between God's written word and God's speaking Voice, which he says predates the Bible by countless centuries and is "that Voice which has not been silent since the dawn of creation," but still sounds throughout the universe.

About this Voice he makes a bold claim: it is his belief that "every good and beautiful thing" that man has created is in response to it. No one is excluded: "The moral philosophers who dreamed their high dreams of virtue, the religious thinkers who speculated about God and immortality, the poets and artists who created out of common stuff pure and lasting beauty: how can we explain them? It is not enough to say simply, 'It was genius.' What then is genius? Could it be that a genius is a man haunted by the speaking Voice, laboring and striving like one possessed to achieve ends which he only vaguely understands?"

He then gives the speaking Voice a name, and calls her Wisdom. Tozer and I had used different words, had taken different paths, but we both ended up on the doorstep of the same house.

My delight at our mutual discovery was short-lived. Tozer has converted our doorstep into a soapbox to make another bold claim. He is sure humanity has gone astray in its response to Wisdom. We have become men of science, he insists; we respond to the speaking Voice without awe. We examine and dissect; we do not kneel and adore. Devoid of reverence for God's speaking Voice, we are no better than (and I'll use my own example here) a medical student who looks at God and sees a flying brain. Tozer wishes again for awe; in fact, he wishes *only* for awe. What I wish is that I could share with him what I've learned through the writing of this book: it's not necessary to choose. Without a spirit-science divide, with a true picture of creativity, we can *both* examine *and* adore. Holy curiosity carries in itself the seeds of both: holy, so that we adore; curiosity, so that we examine. It requires both. Wisdom demands both.

Discovering this was the task set before me two years ago when I first began to unravel my dream. But I didn't undertake the task alone, and now that it is completed, I'm especially grateful for those who played a special role in drawing me to its conclusion.

My first acknowledgment goes to two teachers, not Mrs. Biller and Smelly Nelly (since their contributions have already been noted), but to Katie O'Connell Gregg and to the late John Godar. Miss O'Connell, as she was known then, was my Catholic school English teacher, the very first to nurture my "delicate little plant." She also encouraged her students to keep "paragraph notebooks," writing journals housed in black-and-white composition books. I still use one to this day. John Godar was my high school Honors English teacher after Nelly and while he needled me mercilessly, he made me a better writer, and through our ten years of correspondence that followed high school until his death, he made me a better person.

To the faculty and staff of the University of Mary Washington, who not only allowed me to teach a class devoted entirely to creativity but gave me free rein to design its content. And to my fearless students, for their energy and passion and insatiable curiosity.

To Sealy Yates and Jeana Ledbetter, who first heard this book idea in a crowded New York City convention hall and who later became my agents and my friends.

To my mother, Carmela Christin, for her patronage in the truest sense of the word, and to my father- and mother-in-law, James and Cenia Hollingsworth, for their care and attention every step of the way.

To Dr. Keith Rogers, for his life's work connecting students with their gifts. At first delighted to meet the man behind the work, now I am privileged to call you my friend.

To Martha Bennett, who said just the right thing at just the right time. There is no way for me to adequately thank you for bringing these dry bones back to life.

To Christian Amondson and James Stock of Wipf and Stock Publishers, for their infinite patience and stubborn confidence that meaningful books always find their audience.

To Dr. Robin Parry, my editor extraordinaire, for his intellect and wit and for the most invigorating exchanges I've ever had with a book editor.

Finally, I owe every creative impulse I have to Emily, my muse of dancing; to Jonathan, my muse of sacred song; and to Jeff, my muse of love.

Grateful acknowledgment is made to the following:

Giovanni Maria Pala for permission to reproduce the image of *The Last Supper* with musical notations (copyright by Giovanni Maria Pala, from the book *Leonardo da Vinci—il mistero di un uomo*).

Paul and Gail Dennison for permission to reproduce Brain Gym® movements.

Dr. Keith Rogers for permission to reproduce the Rogers Indicator of Multiple Intelligences.

The Open University for permission to use the mind-map image in chapter 10.